MORE SERIOUS

FUN

MORE SERIOUS FUN

David R. Veerman

VICTOR BOOKS ®

A DIVISION OF SCRIPTURE PRESS PUBLICATIONS INC.
USA CANADA ENGLAND

All Bible quotations, unless otherwise indicated, are from the *Holy Bible, New International Version,* © 1973, 1978, 1984, International Bible Society. Used by permission of Zondervan Bible Publishers. Verses marked TLB are taken from *The Living Bible,* © 1971, Tyndale House Publishers, Wheaton, IL 60189. Used by permission. Other quotations are from J.B. Phillips: *The New Testament in Modern English,* Revised Edition, © J.B. Phillips, 1958, 1960, 1972, permission of Macmillan Publishing Co. and Collins Publishers.

Library of Congress Catalog Number: 88-60214
ISBN: 0-89693-605-8

CONTENTS

1. GAMES 'R' US   9

2. DATING AND BREAKING UP   13

3. PEER PRESSURE   25

4. FAILURE AND REJECTION   33

5. LONELINESS   42

6. DEPRESSION AND SUICIDE   53

7. EMOTIONS   60

8. FAITH AND DOUBTS   70

9. PRAYER AND PRAISE   79

10. WORLD CONCERN AND SOCIAL ACTION   87

11. COMPETITION   99

12. MUSIC   108

13. EASTER   116

DEDICATION

To Ralph, Paul, Barb, and Phil—
brothers and sister who made
growing up fun.

1

GAMES 'R' US!

Games, by definition, are fun; and we need to giggle and guffaw . . . to enjoy. But games also serve a variety of other useful purposes. In them we can relax, unite, unwind, cheer, compete, and learn to win and lose. At a party, games can loosen-up or "break" the crowd and help people get to know each other better. In a class, they can enhance learning by setting the stage for the delivery of the lesson or by actually serving as the teaching vehicle. And games can help build relationships in small groups, in neighborhoods, and at home.

More Serious Fun is a book of games . . . and ideas . . . with a purpose. These "crowd-breakers," "discussion starters," "discussions," and "Bible studies" were written to help deliver profound insights—the life-changing truths of God's Word. Although written with teenagers in mind, these activities can be adapted to almost any size or age group—from church picnics or retreats to special family times.

I have been creating and explaining games for 20 years, for Campus Life high school and junior high meetings, Sunday School classes, church picnics, staff parties, high school assemblies, and all sorts of other settings—and I am convinced of their value. I hope you will be also as you read, adapt, play, and have fun together.

In addition, maybe you will be inspired to dream up your own creative activities. Don't assume that only weird and crazy people invent these games, or that they are written by a group of specially trained professionals. YOU CAN DO IT TOO. Here . . . let's try.

Start by changing a familiar game, like "Ring around the Rosey," and adapting it to your group. One possibility would be to put one of the kids in the middle while the rest of the group forms a circle around him or her. Then have all those in the circle blindfold themselves. Sing the little song and move to the right, but when you get to "all fall down," instead of falling down, everyone should reach and try to *hug* the person in the center. What do you think? Will it work? Maybe not, but it's worth a try. I just thought that up while sitting here writing this—I'm sure you can do better than that.

If you're really ambitious and want to create a lot of games or crowd-breakers (you've been asked to head-up all the games for the block party of you've just been appointed the junior high Sunday School teacher), here's how.

LET YOUR MIND WANDER

Let's assume that you have been given a subject. It could be "peer pressure" for a series with the high school kids or "grace" for an adult Bible study. Or maybe it's just an idea, like "games to help everyone get to know each other." Take a piece of paper and pen, go to a quiet place where you won't be interrupted for a few minutes and write down *everything* that comes to your mind about that subject. For "peer pressure," for example, you could write:

peer	friend	pressure
pressure cooker	under pressure	press
pier	appear	do it
friends	friendly	real friends
giving in	say no	do what's right
right turn	a good turn	right decisions
peering	push/pull	right and wrong
vacuum sealed	Press? Sure!	full-court press

As you can see, we could go on and on. The idea is to let your mind wander and to hitchhike off words, plays on words, associations, etc. Already, many of these words suggest possible activities.

But this is just the beginning. The next step is to let these words and ideas germinate. Keep the list near you and add to it as the day progresses. Watch for items in the newspaper, in magazines, or on television. Eventually you'll have a page full on just *one* subject.

LOOK FOR CLUES

After a few days, go back to your list and look for "clues." These are words, phrases, or ideas which you think may have the seed of a great idea in them. Put an asterisk by them and then try to imagine a game or starter with them. "Full-court press" or "under pressure" may scream out at you, "This would make a *great game!*"

TYPES OF GAMES

One way to kick start your imagination is to consider various types of games and to tie them in to your theme. Here are some possible games:

1. relays
2. contests
3. words/meanings (beginning sounds, rhymes, puns, crosswords, hidden words, scrambled words, "Hangman," invented words, etc.)
4. simulations
5. race (against others, against the clock, against a record, etc.)
6. children's games
7. achievements/tasks (group rhythms, songs, accomplishments, etc.)
8. riddles

9. puzzles
10. charades/impressions
11. sounds (cheers, raps, etc.)
12. hunts/clues
13. talks
14. technology (strobe light, black light, computer, calculator, etc.)
15. sports

RESOURCES

Consider your resources as you begin to imagine and create. First, remember your location. If, for example, you will be in a forest preserve, try to use the natural strengths of that environment. And there are other resources to consider. Some of these are:

1. tape recordings
2. records
3. radio
4. television
5. video tapes
6. books
7. magazines and newspapers
8. photographs
9. songs
10. movies
11. plays and skits

ACTIVITIES

Add to this creative mix possible types of activities you could use. These could include:

1. games (see above)
2. fill-in-the-blanks
3. plays/melodramas/skits
4. songs
5. discussions
6. quizzes
7. puzzles
8. symbols
9. drawings
10. lists and charts
11. sculptures
12. poems and stories
13. videotape/movie/slides
14. crafts
15. projects
16. puppets
17. role plays
18. object lessons
19. case studies
20. acrostics
21. collages/montages
22. mobiles

MATERIALS

By now, you should be overflowing with ideas. But to further spur your imagination, think of all the possible materials that you could use. Especially be on the lookout for different or unique materials (e.g., the hole-punched edges of computer paper, "Slime," leftover wallpaper, etc.). Here are some possibilities. Each of these could birth a hundred ideas.

1. rubber bands
2. Styrofoam
3. candles and/or wax
4. pencils and pens
5. cards/cardboard/poster board

6. paper
7. stones/twigs/leaves/cones
8. straws
9. food (Gummi Bears, marshmallows, cereal, jello, whipped cream, licorice, etc.)
10. crayons and markers
11. chalk and board
12. string/yarn/thread
13. spools
14. wire/hangers
15. hands/fingers/feet/toes
16. shaving cream and makeup
17. toilet paper
18. wallpaper/construction paper/crepe paper
19. nails/screws/pins/clips
20. clothes (belts, hats, shoes/boots, ties, gloves, etc.)
21. cotton balls
22. boxes
23. jewelry
24. clay/Play Doh
25. balloons
26. marbles
27. cellophane tape/masking tape/duct tape
28. clothes pins
29. money

Now you should have plenty to think about—in fact, your mind should be humming with activity. (I think I can hear it now.) And if you really want to have fun, bounce your ideas off another person and watch the creative juices flow.

BUILDING A MEETING

Here's one final consideration—be sure to remember the objective of each activity as you invent and then use it. If, for example, the goal is simply to have fun, then the "title" of the game is probably all you'll need to tie it into the theme of the evening, party, or meeting. But be sure it really is fun. (We call these *crowd-breakers*.)

If, on the other hand, the purpose of the activity is to set the stage for a teaching, make sure that it does just that, and don't let the fun detract from your ultimate goal. (We call these *discussion starters*.)

Going back to the subject of "peer pressure," we could create a crowd-breaker which would involve building a "pier" to withstand certain pressures. This pier could be made of paper or people and could involve the whole group or competition among teams.

One discussion starter could be a quiz with rhyming riddles, all of which related to the subject. Another one could be a video tape, produced earlier, which featured humorous and serious peer pressure situations.

I think you get the idea.

But hey . . . now it's time to have fun . . . and to get serious!

Dave Veerman

2

DATING AND BREAKING UP

CROWD-BREAKERS

Ad ■ Distribute paper and pens and ask everyone to write a newspaper advertisement of 15 words or less for the girl or guy of their dreams. Collect these unique ads and read them aloud.

All in Your Mind ■ This is a skit in which a boy goes to a hypnotist to improve his dating life. The hypnotist puts him under and gives him detailed instructions on how to talk to his date, converse with her father, open the door, eat at the restaurant, etc. After each one, the hypnotized boy repeats back the instruction verbatim. The hypnotist tells him to remember everything when he awakes and then snaps him out of it. The next scene is the date, but because the events happen out of order, the boy does everything wrong. For example, the father answers the door, so the boy has to talk to him first and gives the speech he learned for talking to the girl. Then they go to a movie and have popcorn instead of going to a restaurant, etc.

Blind Date ■ Choose two boys and two girls (or more couples if you want to make this competitive). Designate parts of the room as "rooms" on the date. Explain that one of the boys and one of the girls will be blindfolded and go on a "date" in the room. They will be guided verbally by the other boy and girl through their blind date. The rooms on the date can be the girl's home (boy must climb steps, ring bell, greet father, compliment girl, and escort her to the car); the car—a wagon pulled by a tricycle (boy must seat girl and "drive" them both to the restaurant); and the restaurant (they must pour Coke and drink it, eat cake, etc.). As a competitive event, have another set of couples repeat the procedure—the best time wins.

Candy Kiss Hunt ■ Purchase a bag of Hershey's Kisses wrapped in the red and green foil. Insert a numbered slip of paper inside each wrapping. Make sure you have two of every number, and put one in a "green" kiss and the other in a "red" one (designate one color for boys and the other one for girls). Hide the candies around the room, making sure that none are in sight. Explain about the colored kisses and that each person can only have one. Also tell them about the numbers and that they should find their partners (the other person with the same number). Then have them get up and look for the kisses. Use these pairs in other games involving couples.

Couples Scavenger Hunt ■ Divide into boy-girl couples (couples of the same sex will be all right if the numbers are uneven) and have them sit together. You will call out an item, and whichever couple brings it to you first wins that round. They can use the contents of their purses and pockets and anything else they have on them. Possible scavenger items to call could include a shoelace, 97 cents in change, a ticket stub, a picture of a boyfriend or girlfriend, a gift from someone of the opposite sex, etc.

Date Relay ■ Divide into teams and have the teams sit in columns with a blindfolded male representative in front. Give each team a bag containing about 10 items which a girl could use in getting ready for a big date. The bags should contain identical items. At your signal, the last person should reach into the bag, pull out an item, and pass it to the front. The blindfolded boy at the front should then use that item and pass it back. When it reaches the end of the team, another item may be passed and so on until the bag is empty, and the guys are made-up like girls. The first team finished wins. Items could include lipstick, eye shadow, blush, comb, blouse, dress, toothbrush and paste, mouthwash to gargle, perfume, fingernail polish, and fingernail clippers.

Dating Game ■ Choose three dating couples and run this like television's "Newlywed Game." You can use questions like these:
■ What attracted you to him?
■ What will she say is her greatest strength?
■ How long will he say he thinks you will go together?
■ What does he do that really bugs you?
■ On a scale of 1 to 10, rate your last date together.
■ Who does she most resemble—Blondie, Bo Derek, Mother Theresa, Barbara Walters, or Veronica Hammel?
■ Who does he most resemble—Tom Selleck, Sylvester Stallone, Gary Coleman, Billy Graham, Bruce Springsteen, Prince, or Tony Dorsett?

Dear John Letter ■ Divide into teams, seat the teams in circles, and give each team a piece of paper with "Dear John" written on the top. (If players don't know what a "Dear John" letter is, explain that it is a letter in which one person is trying gracefully to break off a relationship with a boyfriend or girlfriend.) Explain that at your signal they should pass the papers clockwise around their circles with each person adding three words to the letter. The paper should move quickly and continue to circle the group until you signal the end. After a few minutes, stop the game, collect the letters, and read them. (You may want to discuss "Dear John" letters which they have received or how people break up with others.)

Dream Girl/Guy ■ Ask for the group to give the parts of speech that you need to fill in the blanks in the paragraphs below. Don't let them know what the stories are about until all the blanks are filled. Then give them the title and read their creations.

DREAM GIRL

The girl of my dreams has _____ (adjective) _____ (color) hair. Her _____ (plural noun) are _____ (color), and when she _____ (verb) them at me, I melt. Her figure is _____ (adjective); her femininity is _____ (adjective). And what a personality! She is _____ (adjective) and has a great sense of _____ (noun). As a matter of fact, she's one of the most _____ (adjective) girls in school. The person most like this dream girl is _____ (name of girl in room).

DREAM GUY

My ideal guy is about _____ (number) feet tall with _____ ("ing" adjective) muscles. Not only is he a great athlete, but he is also a _____ (adjective) student. Last semester, he got _____ (number) A's and only _____ (number) F's. He is always _____ (adjective) and _____ (adjective) and very sensitive to my _____ (plural noun). He spares no expense on our dates—the last one cost $_____ (number) when he took me to _____ (place). As a matter of fact, the one guy who most reminds me of him is _____ (name of guy in room).

Here are a couple of additional scripts to use.

PERFECT GUY

My perfect man is a real _____ (noun). He's about _____ (number) feet tall and has a _____ (adjective) complexion. His hair is _____ (adjective) and _____ (adjective). His sexy eyes are _____ (color). They remind me of _____ (plural noun). His _____ (plural noun) ripple, and he has a _____ (adjective) walk. This dream boat always treats me _____ (adverb); he's so _____ (adjective) and _____ (adjective).

PERFECT GIRL

This perfect girl has beautiful long flowing _____ (noun). When she _____ (verb) her eyes at me, I _____ (verb). She has a perfect figure: _____ (number), _____ (number), _____ (number). She always wears such _____ (adjective) _____ (plural noun) too. . . and what a _____ (noun); her smile _____ (verb) and lights up the room. She is a perfect example of _____ (noun) and _____ (noun).

Egg Juggling ■ Find two or three group members who know how to juggle. Bring them to the front and let them demonstrate their skills using tennis balls. Give each juggler a big round of applause and then explain that you want them to compete in a juggling contest. After they agree, explain that they will be juggling raw eggs. Bring out the eggs and let them begin (three eggs per person). Do one person at a time and count each time an egg is caught in the left hand. A person's turn ends when he or she breaks an egg. (Note: Even very good jugglers have trouble with eggs because of the possibility of breakage. Be sure to protect the floor and furniture.)

Juggling eggs is like dating because even though the idea is not to break up, it seems inevitable.

Finder of Lost Loves ■ This word game would be good for those who come to the meeting early or on time. Give each person a puzzle in which to find the "lost loves." In your puzzle, mix in 9 or 10 dating and love words, hidden among other miscellaneous letters. The words may be written backward, forward, up, down, or diagonally. Be sure to list them on the sheet so the kids will know what to look for. The first person to find all the words wins. Here is a sample puzzle.

```
B A N Y I H L R I G S     Hidden words: BROKEN, LOVE, HEART,
O R B E L E I K L O I     TRUE, JUST FRIENDS, LETTER, DATE,
Y E O F O T J R L S N     GO STEADY, PAIN, HATE, BOY,
A C T K V A R E N T G     GIRL, ME, SINGLE, SOLE
C T R A E H P T O E L
R R C G D N A T P A E
J U S T F R I E N D S
M E D H J K N L Q Y T
```

Flipside ■ Hand out the following list of desirable qualities in a potential mate. Then have everyone write the negative side of each quality. For example, "steady and sure" can also be "slow and boring," and "outgoing and effervescent" can become "flighty and scatterbrained." Afterward, discuss their answers and talk about the implications for choosing or being a good date.

FLIPSIDE

1. beautiful hair —

2. great sense of humor —

3. a good mind, solid thinker —

4. spontaneous and exciting —

5. generous, a big spender —

6. sensitive —

7. musical, very talented —

8. very athletic —

9. a great figure —

10. polite and considerate —

11. quiet and thoughtful —

12. confident and self-assured —

Handle with Care ■ Set up a relay in which teams transport fragile items through an obstacle course. Possible items could include: wet tissue paper supporting a golf ball; a Ping-Pong ball balanced on a piece of cardboard; a spoon carrying a raw egg (an empty shell would be less messy); a balloon held between the knees; a plastic plate balanced on one finger; a cookie held between the elbows; ribbon candy held between the teeth; etc. This relay illustrates how relationships are fragile and must be handled with care.

16

Humpty Dumpty ■ Do this as a contest of speed and dexterity between two volunteers or team representatives (it may also be run as a relay). Explain that you have difficult puzzles for them to assemble—the first one finished will receive a prize and the last one, a penalty.

Seat the two contestants behind a table and give each one a roll of tape and some string to use to hold their "puzzles" together. Explain that when they have finished the first puzzle, you will give them another one and so on until you run out of puzzles. Keep your puzzles in separate bags so the pieces won't get mixed up. Here are possible puzzles, in order of difficulty.

1. a picture from a magazine, cut into 10 pieces
2. "Tinker Toy" or "Lego" pieces with pictures of the finished objects
3. a red, construction paper heart, cut into 15 pieces
4. an apple, cut into sections
5. a banana, peeled (with peel in two parts) and cut into 3 pieces
6. an egg shell, broken into a number of pieces (Use whole eggs with the contents blown out. Carefully break them into pieces as large as possible.)

The point is that after a breakup it's difficult to get together again.

Ideal Date ■ Divide into 10 groups and give each group a "part" of the date. Tell them to write their idea of that specific part of an ideal date. Collect the parts and read them in order. Here are possible date parts: guy (description); guy (clothes); girl (description); girl (clothes); transportation; dinner (menu); dinner (place); main event; event location; date ending.

Love Is Blind ■ Divide into teams and have each team choose a couple (boy and girl) to compete for them. Bring all the couples to the front and blindfold them. Give each couple an identical set of items and explain that, while blindfolded, their job is to get their partners ready for a date—and they have only three minutes to complete the job. The guys' bags should contain lipstick, hairbrush, hairspray, toothpaste and brush, and a necklace. The girls' bags should contain shaving cream and razor (without blade), mouthwash, comb, hairspray, and a neck chain. Say **Go** and watch the fun. Be sure to be prepared for the mess too.

May I Have This Dance? ■ Pair off your group into couples and choose one person in each pair to be the leader. Explain that you are going to have a group dance, so each couple should assume the waltz position. The idea in this dance is for the leader to lead and the follower to follow (this sounds easy enough). Then turn on the tape which you have prepared beforehand and watch the chaos and fun. (Note: The tape should have parts of a number of songs, ranging from easy-listening ballads to hard rock. You may also want to throw in parts of a polka and a waltz.) Whatever the style of music, your couples should dance facing each other in the waltz position. After a few minutes, reverse the leader and follower roles and continue the dance.

Partners ■ Have everyone choose a partner. This should be someone of the opposite sex if possible. Let them chat for a minute or two, then have them sit down, back to back. Emphasize the fact that they must not cheat and then ask the following questions. Give each person 100 points for every correct answer.

1. **Is this person wearing a class ring?**
2. **What is the color of his or her eyes?**
3. **Do his or her shoes tie?**
4. **What is the color of his or her shirt?**

5. Is he or she wearing a watch?
   You may add questions of your own. The person with the most points wins.

Silence Is Broken ■ Before the meeting, tape-record a number of sounds of things breaking. During the meeting, play the tape and have the kids write down what they think the broken items are. Then play the sounds again and give the correct answers. Here are some possible sounds:
- light bulb breaking
- balloon popping
- paper tearing
- twig or pencil snapping
- wave breaking on the shore
- wood being chopped
- promise being broken (verbal—"I'm sorry. . . .")
- heart breaking (sound of crying)
- Styrofoam cup being squashed
- string or thread snapping

   Afterward you could ask, **What does breaking up sound like?**

Strings Attached ■ Put all the girls on one side of the room and all the guys on the other. On the floor between them, place a number of strings. They should be about three feet long and should be crossed but not tangled. Tell each person to pick up an end to a piece of string. At a signal, they should find their respective partners (at the strings' other ends). Next, give them five minutes to discover the following information about each other: middle name, unique or hidden talent, best vacation spent, career goals, last time punished by parents and reason, and favorite dessert. Have them report the most unusual findings to the group. Note: If you prepare the strings ahead of time, lay them on the floor and cover them with a newspaper.

Super Date ■ Promote this activity well. Run it as a version of "The Newlywed Game" with the winning couple receiving a "super date." The contest, then, should involve a series of questions designed to see which couple knows each other best. For the prize, line up the following (get them donated if possible): tuxedo for the guy; a luxury car (limo, etc., driven by a chauffeur or you); flowers; dinner for three (the couple plus you) at a fancy restaurant; theatre or concert tickets; etc.

DISCUSSION STARTERS

Advice ■ Distribute the following worksheet. Have the students check which source they would go to first for advice on each problem. Then discuss who they listen to the most and who they think is right

Problem	Parents	Friend	TV/Movie	Society	God
1. Whom to date					
2. Kissing on a date					
3. Where to go					
4. Going steady					

5. Petting

6. Marriage

7. Sexual intercourse

Assignment ■ Ask your students to talk to their parents during the week about dating. They should ask:
1. How did the parents meet?
2. What attracted them most in the other person?
3. What was the biggest positive surprise in marriage?
4. What was the biggest negative surprise in marriage?
Have the kids come to the next meeting prepared to discuss what they learned.

Blind Date ■ Choose two volunteers who do not know each other (possibly from different schools) to go on a blind date. This truly will be a "blind date" because they both will be blindfolded the entire time. Have the staff chaperone (and guide) pick them up and introduce them to each other, using first names only. Then the guide should take them out to eat at a restaurant like Arby's or Burger King, and then to a park where they can spend time talking and playing a game (if there's snow, they could build a snowman). The whole date should last only about two hours. Then they should be brought to the meeting (on time), where the blindfolds will be removed and they will discuss their experience. You should also discuss how dating is usually based on looks and on what others think (and how this experience differs).

Breaking Up Is Hard to Do ■ Choose a few guys and girls to role play the following situations:
■ You have been dating steadily for three months. Lately, however, things have been a little stale and you (the girl) have decided that you should break up. You still feel the same way about him, but you want the freedom to date around. The two of you are talking about your relationship.
■ You (boy) have finally gotten up the courage to ask her out, and so you call her up and ask. You (girl) don't want to go out with him, and so you make up excuses.
■ You (girl) have had a few dates with him and really like him a lot. Lately, however, he has been sort of avoiding you in the halls. You sit down next to him at lunch and begin to talk. You (boy) think she's OK, but you're really not that interested.
■ You (girl) are trying to tell him that you want to be "just friends."
After each role play, discuss how realistic the situation and the acting were and what people can do to make dating and boy-girl relationships less tense and pressure-filled.

Cards ■ If your meeting about sex has been quite heavy and personal, you will want to provide the opportunity for kids to receive counseling. Distribute cards and have everyone write their reactions to the topic of the meeting. Then have them write "yes" if they or friends have been involved in a "date rape" situation (the boy forced himself on the girl). This doesn't mean that intercourse necessarily happened, but that the pressure was there. Then ask them to write their names if they want to get together for a personal appointment with you or another sponsor to talk over their feelings and to get help. Assure them that no one else will see these cards and that you will respect their privacy. Collect the cards and put them out of sight until you can read them later.

Case Study ■ Write a case study of the typical, very serious, high school romance (e.g., John and Suzie are in love, and they've pledged to "love each other forever"—their names are carved on trees all over town. A silly misunderstanding leads to an argument which eventually leads to their breakup. After the breakup, they won't talk to each other, they say they hate each other, and they always put each other down with friends, etc.).

Read the case study and then ask:

■ **Do you know of a similar situation?** (This can be answered by a show of hands.)
■ **Why do couples become so hateful?**
■ **How can this whole scene be avoided?**
■ **What are the differences between those couples who can break up in a friendly manner (and still be friends) and those who "hate" each other?**
■ **Why do couples make the commitment of going "steady" in the first place (almost like marriage)?**

Dear Best Buddy ■ Give everyone a piece of paper and a pencil and explain that each person has a letter to write. Here are the situations:

■ Girls—Your best friend has been asked to go to a hotel party. She really doesn't want to go, either with the person who has asked her or to the party, but she wants to be popular and accepted by the group. Write good advice to her concerning what she should do and what she should tell the guy who asked her.
■ Guys—Your best friend has told you that all of his buddies want him to go to that hotel party and chip in for the room, but he really doesn't want to go. Write and tell him what he should do.

Make sure the letters are anonymous. Collect, read, and discuss them.

Double Standard ■ Choose two volunteers to participate in a role play. Be sure to have the necessary props on hand. In this role play, the guy will be playing the part of the girl and the girl, the part of the guy. Here's the situation. The guy (played by the girl, who will be using lines she has heard) is trying to ask out a girl over the phone. The girl (played by the guy) doesn't want to go out with him and is turning him down without lying. The guy persists.

Afterward, discuss how realistic the scene was.

Interviews ■ Divide into couples. Then give each person a pencil and a piece of paper and tell them that they have three minutes (90 seconds each) to interview each other about what they look for in someone to date. Have them report the results of the interviews. Compile a list and discuss the differences and similarities and why they look for what they do.

Ideal Index ■ Divide into boys and girls and send them to separate rooms. Make sure that each group has a leader (an adult sponsor would be good). This leader should distribute cards on which the following is written:

IDEAL INDEX
What is your idea of the ideal date? Answer with a person or statement.
BODY like . . .
MIND like . . .

SKIN . . .
LAUGHTER . . .
EYES . . .
VOICE . . .
PERSONALITY . . .
OTHER . . .

After everyone has filled out these cards, the leaders should collect them and have a brief discussion about why they wrote what they did. Then, while still in separate rooms, the leaders should lead a discussion on the following questions (and have someone record the answers):

1. How do you experience disrespect from members of the opposite sex?
2. What words imply disrespect? Why?
3. What actions imply disrespect? Why?

Bring the whole group back together and have each leader read some of the "Ideal Index" cards. This will be light, so don't discuss the answers. Then have the leaders read the answers to their questions about disrespect. This is very important, so make sure that everyone takes the answers seriously. As you proceed, be sure to ask why we, as men and women, are hateful or disrespectful toward each other and how we can show more respect. Compare the "disrespect list" with their "ideal index," and ask where respect fits into the index.

Prayer ■ Because much guilt can surface in a discussion about dating and sex, spend time in silent prayer. Encourage everyone to use this time to talk to God about their guilt or to ask for help for themselves or those who are in destructive dating relationships.

Another way to facilitate this would be to have each person go to a different part of the room or building to spend time alone, talking over this whole area with God, asking for His forgiveness and direction.

Questions ■ Hand out index cards on which kids can write any questions about dating, date abuse, or breaking up they would like you to attempt to answer at your next meeting.

DISCUSSIONS

Breaking Up ■ Begin by asking how many can think of a couple who has broken up recently (ask for a show of hands). Then say: **Now don't raise your hands, but how many of you have had the experience yourselves? It's no fun when it happens to you.** Then ask:

■ **What are some reasons for the breakups you have observed or experienced?**
■ **How do couples break up? What lines are used?**
■ **Can people who used to be serious be "just friends" after a breakup? Why or why not? How?**

Cruel and Unusual Punishment ■ Use this as a wrap-up or as a discussion guide.

Someone has said that dating is "cruel and unusual punishment"—yet it is the only "mating ritual" we have. It's kind of scary, isn't it, to think that our dates prepare us for marriage? Of course, some people go in totally blind and are surprised at what they get. Some look for a person who will meet their emotional needs. Others use the trial-and-error method. If their marriage doesn't work out, they divorce and try again (until they get it right). Still others play the waiting game, expecting God to drop "Mr. or Ms. Right" in their laps. Most of us don't like the old idea of parents arranging our weddings, but maybe it would be a lot better than these other ways of choosing mates.

And then there is the whole matter of love. This is a subject for another whole meeting. Here let me just say that our idealized, romantic ideas of love tend to complicate the process. In America, we believe that *you marry the person you love.* In reality, no matter how you choose a mate, *you have to learn to love the person you marry.*

God wants us to take seriously this whole area of dating, love, and marriage. It's not a game, and marriage is the most important decision a person can make after the decision to accept Christ as Saviour.

Are you dating with a purpose? Have you involved God in the process? Remember, He loves you and wants to be part of every decision you make.

Dating ■ Ask:
■ How do you decide whom you will date?
■ Why do most high school couples stay together?
■ What is the purpose of dating?
■ How can dating prepare you for marriage?

Games ■ Ask:
■ Is our system of dating good or bad? Why?
■ Which is easier, asking someone out or being asked out? Why?
■ What kind of "games" are played on dates? (E.g., being cool, saying the right lines, trying to find out what the other person thinks of you, etc.)
■ Have you ever heard of "date abuse"? What is it?
■ What is the answer to "date abuse"?

Loving the Wrong Type ■ Ask:
■ It is said that love and compatibility are different. What do you think that means?
■ What is the difference between love and dependence?
■ What kind of qualities should you look for in the one you marry?

Mate Meeting ■ Ask:
■ When do you think you will meet your "mate"? Describe the situation.
■ How will you know that this is "the one"?
■ What can you do now to help prepare you for this future scenario?

Strengths and Weaknesses ■ Ask:
■ What are some strengths in people you know?
■ What do you think it means that a person's strength is his or her weakness?
■ How would this relate to marriage?

The Pain ■ Use this outline as a discussion guide or for a wrap-up.
1. Often we set ourselves up for painful breakups because we . . .
   a. rush into relationships

b. expect too much from the other person—we're unrealistic or make too many demands
c. commit ourselves too soon
d. don't allow the relationship to grow
e. get involved in an unbalanced relationship—emotional release, heavy sex, etc.

2. Instead, we should . . .
   a. proceed slowly
   b. become friends first—get to know the other person
   c. date a variety of people in a variety of situations
   d. be honest about our feelings and take it a day at a time
   e. resist using the other person to meet our needs or playing on their emotions

3. And, most important of all, we should let Christ control this area of our lives by . . .
   a. commiting each person and situation to Him
   b. acting in love toward our dates
   c. responding in love after any breakup

BIBLE STUDIES

Bible Dates ■ Work through the following passages together or break into groups and give each group a separate passage to discuss.

1. Read Genesis 2:18-25 and ask:
   ■ **Do you know anyone who expects to find his or her spouse this way? Explain.**
   ■ **What do you think the phrase "made for each other" means?**
   ■ **Do you think God has one person picked out for you? Why or why not?**
2. Read Genesis 14:1-67 (or summarize) and ask:
   ■ **How did Isaac meet Becky?**
   ■ **Have your parents ever tried to match you with anyone? How did you respond?**
   ■ **What advantages would there be in having your marriage "arranged"?**
   ■ **Where does love fit into all of this?**
3. Read 2 Samuel 11:1-5 and ask:
   ■ **What attracted David to his "date"?**
   ■ **What TV shows have featured similar scenarios?**
   ■ **What are the disadvantages to meeting this way?**
   ■ **Where does love fit into all of this?**

Respect ■ Have someone read John 13:35 aloud. Have others read 1 Corinthians 13 and other passages about love. Then ask how these passages relate to dating. Emphasize that each person is responsible, before God, for his or her actions; that is, as Christians we must obey God, and Christian love is an action, not a feeling. Challenge them that respect for each other is not optional, it is a requirement, and that it is active, not passive. Give everyone a sheet of paper and have them write the words or phrases from the Bible which apply directly to them in their relationships with members of the opposite sex. After a minute or so, explain that they may have to go to certain people and ask for forgiveness; certainly their actions must change.

Where Is the Love? ■ Look up together the following passages on love. Read

them and then ask how they relate to dating and breaking up.
1. Matthew 22:36-39 (love your neighbor)
2. Matthew 5:43-47 (love your enemies)
3. 1 Corinthians 13:4-7, 13 (love is the greatest)
4. 1 John 4:7-8 (love comes from God)

Ask your students how they can respond in a loving way in a breakup instead of with hatred.

3

PEER PRESSURE

CROWD-BREAKERS

Acting School ■ Before the meeting, prepare slips of paper with the names of famous personalities or "types of people" written on them. During the meeting, using teams, have each team send a representative to draw a slip naming a person or type which he or she must act out for the group. This is like charades in that no words may be spoken, and the only clue which can be given is whether it is a "person" or "type." After that, the actor must play the role while his or her team tries to guess the correct answer. Keep track of the time it takes each team—the lowest total time wins. Here are some possible personalities and types; you can add names of people from school and church:

Personalities	*Types*
Sylvester Stallone	jock
Bill Cosby	nerd
Michael J. Fox	wimp
Max Headroom	"space cadet"
Tom Cruise	party animal
Madonna	druggie
Nancy Reagan	punk
the school principal	"in crowd"
the football coach	country
Michael Jordan	tough guy/girl
Eric Dickerson	conceited
Smurfette	shy
Mr. Rogers	student body president
Pee Wee Herman	drunk with hangover

Tie in to the theme of peer pressure by noting how "types" can often be identified by their common actions or style of dress.

Domino Effect ■ Bring a number of boxes of dominoes and create a group domino sculpture. When you're finished, take a picture of it, and then count down and push the first domino—and watch them fall.

Note: If you want to use this as a discussion starter, ask: **What does the "domino effect" mean? How does this operate in your school? When have you felt like a domino?**

Lip Sync ■ "Lip-syncing" (a person or group mimes and synchronizes the movement of their mouths and lips with a popular song) is quite popular (there's even a television show featuring it—"Putting on the Hits"). This will take preparation, but it can be a lot of fun. Have a couple of acts ready to go and spotlight them in the meeting. If you wish, use this as a springboard to introduce the subject of imitation and peer pressure.

Lost in the Crowd ■ Mark out a course with masking tape on the floor. You may want to position various penalties along the course or simply use a point system and run this as a contest. Either way, choose three or four "volunteers." Explain that you will take them from the room. Then they will enter, one at a time, blindfolded, and try to walk the taped course (one foot in front of the other). They will know where to walk from the sounds of the rest of the crowd lined along the course. If they should take a step straight ahead, the group will hum quietly. If they should step to the right, the group will hum a higher pitch, and to the left, a lower pitch. The more severe the angle of the turn to be taken, the higher (or lower) the pitch. At the end of the course (or time limit), the blindfold will be removed, and they will be told their score (or receive their penalties and/or rewards). Note: While they are walking, you should act as the "choir director" for the crowd.

Ping-Pong Blow ■ This may be done with everyone or as a round-robin tournament with teams, depending on the size of the group. Use a Ping-Pong table if possible, but a hard floor with boundaries marked as though it were a table will also work. Arrange your two teams around the table, one on each side and no one at either end. Place the Ping-Pong ball in the middle. At your signal, the teams should try to blow the ball down the table and off their opponent's side (or across the boundary line on the floor). No hands may be used; and when the ball goes out of bounds on a side, it should be placed back in the middle of the table at the point where it went out.

This experience can relate to James 1:5-8, which describes a double-minded person blown about; often we feel that way when trying to please everyone.

Reversal ■ This will emphasize the importance of turning peer pressure around.

Divide into teams and have each team choose two representatives who will act as a "worker" and a "teller." Explain that the goal of the workers is to complete a simple task which you will tell to the respective tellers. The tellers will shout the directions. The first worker to complete the task will win. The only catch is that the tellers' instructions will be exactly opposite what they should do; the workers should listen to what the tellers say and do exactly the opposite.

You can give all the teams the same task or different, but similar ones. Continue for as many rounds as you have time. Here are some possible tasks:
■ Walk backward to the far wall; turn counterclockwise two times; print your name

on a piece of paper, last name first; and then crawl forward back to the starting line.

- Get as low as possible; stretch as high as possible; say, "Wow," as loudly as you can; say, "All right," as quietly as you can; shake hands with everyone on your team whose last names begin with *W* or below in the alphabet.

Squeeze Play ■ Divide into teams. Bring out an inflated innertube and explain that the goal of this game is to see which team can get all its members through the tube the fastest, one at a time. Time the teams and record their times. Then announce that for the second round, they must go through the tube by twos. For the third and final round, they can go through with any number at a time (allow time for them to determine a strategy).

Note: If your group is too small for teams, do this as a task to be accomplished by the whole group or as a contest between twos or threes, depending on the size of the tube, where they have to begin with the tube at the floor around their ankles and move it up over their heads without using any hands.

This can relate to Romans 12:1-2 in the Phillips version: "Don't let the world around you squeeze you into its own mold." Ask about the kind of molds they see in school and when and why they feel squeezed.

The Big Squeeze ■ Bring a box of lemons and limes, two pairs of boxing gloves (or heavy work gloves), and two tall glasses. Choose two competitors (individuals or team representatives—use two guys; then repeat with two girls). Explain that they will be competing in "the big squeeze" and will be making homemade "limon" (a la Sprite). The object is to see who can squeeze the most lemon and lime juice into the glass in three minutes while wearing the boxing gloves. The loser will have to drink the winner's glass of juice.

This illustrates how we can feel squeezed, emptied, and cast aside by others. When have they felt like a squeezed lemon?

Who Sez ■ Run this like the children's game "Simon Says," except that you should substitute your name for "Simon." Then run the group through their paces, seeing who can follow your instructions accurately. Here are some possible instructions:
- stand up
- turn to the right
- wave your hand
- stop waving
- pat the person to your immediate right on the back
- stop patting
- hum softly . . . louder . . . louder . . . louder . . . higher
- stop humming
- recite your favorite poem
- stop reciting
- hold your breath
- start breathing naturally again
- bend at the waist
- put your left hand on your right ankle
- stand on your right leg only
- sit on the floor

Remember to begin most of the directions with "_____ says," but be sure to do others without any preface. When the game is over, you can ask the kids if they ever do things just because "So-and-so" says.

DISCUSSION STARTERS

Application ■ To end a meeting, distribute paper and pencils and give everyone a minute or two to think of one or two kids who always seem to give in to peer pressure. Have the students write the names of those people on their papers and commit themselves to pray each day for those people and about how to respond to them.

Assignment ■ To end a meeting, tell everyone to find another person to make a covenant with. They should promise to each other that:
■ they will pray for each other every day
■ they will affirm each other whenever possible
■ they will correct, in love, each other when necessary
■ they will renew this covenant every two weeks

Conforming ■ Tell the story of a high school person you know who has a problem with conformity—someone who has tried to fit in to a variety of groups at school, without success. Then ask:
■ **When have you tried to fit into a specific group? What happened?**
■ **Do you ever feel as though you don't belong to any specific group? But which group do others think you belong to? Why?**
■ **When have you wanted to belong to a certain clique so much that you would do almost anything to get in?**
■ **Who is the "in" crowd in your school? Are you in the "in crowd"? What makes them "in" anyway?**

Fashion Show ■ Before the meeting, line up three boys and three girls to act as models, wearing the latest styles of clothes and modeling them for the rest of the group.

During the meeting, announce that you will be having a fashion show. Clear a path down the middle for a "runway," turn on soft background music, and bring your "models" in, one by one. As they model their outfits, be sure to have them stop at various points as you describe what they are wearing.

After this serious fashion show, break into three groups and tell them to dress one of their members in the "fashion of the future." Give each team newspapers, cloth, various pieces of clothing, hats, accessories, pins, and makeup, and allow 5 to 10 minutes for them to choose their person and design and dress him or her. Then have the second part of your fashion show.

Afterward ask:
■ **How important is "fashion" to you?**
■ **Who sets the standards for what we wear? Is that right? Why or why not?**
■ **What are other fashions besides clothes, hairstyles, and makeup? Which of these are "unchristian"?**
■ **How does Romans 12:2, where God tells us not to copy the behavior and customs of the world, apply to fashion?**

Group Think ■ Take three people out of the room, ostensibly to participate in another game. Use these kids as the "guinea pigs." The idea is to use group pressure to see if these people can be convinced to choose a wrong answer.

While the volunteers are out of the room, clue your crowd that during the discussion time later on, you will be asking three questions involving "a." "b." and "c." answers. The correct answer to the first question will be "c." and they should vote for "c." The correct answer to the second question will also be "c." but they should vote for "b." The correct answer to the third question will obviously be "b." but they should choose "a." (To make it a little more realistic, you may want to select a couple of kids to choose the other wrong answer.)

Here are three possible questions. You may be able to think of better ones. Write them on a large piece of poster board.

1. Fill in the missing number in this series: 3, 9, 27, ___, 243.
   a. 45
   b. 75
   c. 81

2. Which figure has the most area?

   a.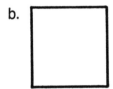

   b.

   c.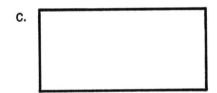

3. Which line is longer?

   a.

   b.

   c.

Bring in your contestants and have them compete in another game. Then, during the discussion time, bring out the poster board and have the crowd vote for their answers by raising their hands. During the questioning and voting, watch carefully how your "guinea pigs" react and answer. Without giving away what you've done, ask one or two of them why they chose their specific answers. Then explain the trick—that they were set up—and ask them:

■ **How did you feel when you knew the right answer but saw everyone else voting for the wrong answer?**

■ **Who influenced you the most and why?**

Note: Be sure to affirm them for being good sports and give a personal illustration about when you gave in to peer pressure.

Ask the whole group:

- **When have you felt like this?**
- **What are some typical pressures you face?** (E.g., drinking and drugs, cheating, gossiping, having sex, etc.)
- **What would it take for you to make the right decisions?**

Man on the Street ■ In the weeks preceding your meeting, have a couple of students record interviews with several of their classmates (these should not be their close friends) about their views on a various subjects such as drinking, cheating in school, abortion, sex, dating, and others. Keep those interviewed anonymous.

Play the tapes at the meeting and discuss the prevailing views on each subject. Then ask your students how the views expressed match with their friends' ideas—and with theirs. Discuss how they would answer some of their classmates and friends who try to pressure them into believing, saying, or doing something which is against their beliefs, values, or morals.

Persuaders ■ Choose four very persuasive individuals and place them in the corners of the room. Have everyone else leave the room. Let them reenter one person at a time, blindfolded, and stand in the center of the room. (If you have a large group, you may do this with up to four at a time.) The idea is for each person in the corners, the persuaders, to persuade the blindfolded individual to come to his or her corner. Each person should take no more than 30 seconds to make the choice. After a person has chosen a corner, he or she should join the persuader in trying to persuade the next one to choose their corner. After everyone has chosen, ask:

- What kind of tactics were used to try to persuade you to come to a corner?
- Persuaders, what was your strategy? When there were more than one in a corner, what kind of strategy did you use and why?
- Why did you choose your corner? What persuaded you?
- When do you feel pulled or persuaded in school? With your friends?
- What pressures have you used to persuade others to join your group or to go along with the group's ideas—obvious or subtle?
- What drew you to your group?

DISCUSSIONS

Belonging ■ Use the following outline as a guide for a discussion or wrap-up.

Problems of Belonging
1. Feeling the pressure of the expectations of others—people do look on the outward appearance, and often they are looking for the wrong things.
2. Doing what others want—the expectations that others have for us are their problem; giving in or catering to those expectations is our problem. Note: God also has expectations for us, but they are quite different from most of the group's. God's expectations are always helpful and healthy.
3. Having wrong goals—the group will often try to define who we are and what we should do; but why should our values and what we are be decided by a group of insecure people who are also looking for who they are?
4. Being subject to group thinking—often the demands and standards of a group are different from the individual preferences of group members. When this occurs, what happens to the individual?

Alternative Ways of Belonging

1. Christians should have the reputation of loving each other across all kinds of "barriers"—all kinds of people are included in the body of Christ.
2. True Christianity has to be accepted and applied by individuals—a group faith that is only a group faith is not good enough.
3. Christians should continue to reach out in love to others, especially to those whom the world has rejected (see Matthew 25:35-40).

Masks ■ Ask: **What kinds of "masks" do kids wear at school to hide who they really are? At parties? In the neighborhood?** Suggest the following and a few others: the "Escape Mask," the "Aloof or Put-down Mask," the "Clown or Distractor Mask," and "Clique Mask" (these are taken from *Real Friends* by Barbara Varenhorst [Harper and Row]). Then discuss the masks that your students use most often and ask why they wear masks at all.

BIBLE STUDIES

Resisting the Pressure ■ Assign the following verses to individual students. Have the verses read, one at a time, and ask the questions listed beneath. Then make each point given below the questions.

1. Psalm 139:1-18
   - **What part has God already played in our lives? What does God think of us?**
   - **What does this passage imply about our identity?**
   - POINT: To resist peer pressure, we must know *who* we are as special and unique creations of God.
2. 1 Corinthians 6:19-20
   - **Why should we glorify God with our actions?**
   - **What price was paid for us? Why is this significant?**
   - POINT: To resist peer pressure, we must know *whose* we are—children of God, bought by our loving Father with the price of Jesus' death.
3. Matthew 6:31-34; Hebrews 12:1-2
   - **How do these verses suggest that we can resist peer pressure? How would that work?**
   - **The emphasis is on our goal and our focus—what should these be?**
   - POINT: To resist peer pressure, we must be convinced that God's way is best, and we must keep our eyes on Christ.
4. Luke 12:51-53; John 15:18-20
   - **What may be the result of our centering our lives on Christ?**
   - **When have you been "persecuted" for your faith? Do you ever "sell out" when the going gets tough? When?**
   - POINT: To resist peer pressure, we must recognize that opposition is the common experience of one who follows Christ.
5. Philippians 4:4-7
   - **What will be the result of trusting in Christ instead of our circumstances?**
   - **How is this related to resisting peer pressure?**
   - POINT: To resist peer pressure, we must be people of prayer—praying for stength, for fellow believers, and for those who abuse us.

Standing Alone ■ Explain that peer pressure is a difficult problem faced by all of us regardless of our age. We all can be bent out of shape trying to please the crowd—it's not easy being an individual, standing alone.

Then have someone read Romans 12:2 aloud. Ask:

- **What does it mean to "conform to the world"? What is "the world"?**
- **What does it mean to be "transformed"? What is a "renewed mind"?**
- **How will the "renewing of our minds" help us resist conforming?**
- **How is all this connected to doing what God wants—His "good, pleasing, and perfect will"?**

Have another student read 1 John 2:15-17 aloud. Ask:

- **What categories of things does this passage say are "in the world"?**
- **How are these values reflected in your school?**
- **Compare the world's values with God's values.**
- **How should this passage and the one we read in Romans help you to stand for Christ?**

Next, hand out cards and pens and have everyone write down two steps they will take to build their defenses against peer pressure. Then have them get into pairs, share what they've written on their cards, and pray for each other.

4

FAILURE AND REJECTION

CROWD-BREAKERS

Bumbles, Fumbles, and Mumbles ■ This is a short film about failure. It features a variety of hilarious sports mess-ups and has a brief message about learning from our failures. It is available to rent or purchase from CAMFEL Productions, 136 Olive Avenue, Monrovia, CA 91016.

Chosen ■ Before the meeting, choose two captains and explain to them that to begin the meeting they will choose their teams for the first couple of games. After a coin toss to see who chooses first, they will alternate choosing team members. Instead of choosing the biggest, strongest, fastest, and most popular kids first, however, they should reverse the process without making it obvious that they are doing so. (They should use a random selection process but make sure that those who normally would be chosen first are taken last.)

After forming the teams, if you have room, play a game of "blind volleyball" (the net is covered by blankets so you can't see the other team; no spiking is allowed) or full participation volleyball (five different team members must hit the ball in each volley). If room is a problem, play charades with popular song titles or hold an indoor scavenger hunt.

Use the "choosing experience" later in your discussion or wrap-up.

Group Hurts ■ Pass out index cards and have all your group members write, anonymously, something that has been done to them which still hurts. Make sure they write these in such a way that no personalities can be identified. Then collect, shuffle, and read the papers aloud. Comment on the types of hurts experienced by the group, the kinds of hurts that were written by more than one person, the fact that these only scratch the surface, and the fact that these hurts are still felt after days, months, or even years. Also point out how many relate to feelings of failure or being rejected. Then discuss forgiveness in general, how we can help others who are struggling, and how we can bring these feelings to God for healing.

Imagination ■ Tell the group to use their imaginations to experience the situations which you will be giving them. They should act out the part as they imagine themselves in your stories. Read these situations with appropriate flourish, and allow time for everyone to react.

■ **Rocky X**—You are Rocky Balboa, the heavyweight champion of the world, and it's the fight of the century. You leave your dressing room and stride confidently to the ring, waving to all your fans. Ducking under the ropes, you dance around and go to your corner.

Next, you shed your robe, walk to the center of the ring, and shake hands with your opponent—the wild "Mr. U," an alien from Russia. The bell rings, and the fight begins. Jab with your left—again—again—now a sharp right—a jab—cover up—he's coming in—he hit you in the body—you backpedal, countering with a right—he's coming on and connects with a left and a right—you're hurt—another shot to the head—you're down . . . and out!

■ **Mr./Ms. Cool**—It's lunch, and you're carrrying your tray from the line, avoiding assorted freshmen on the way to your table. Then you spot her (or him), across the room, the new girl (guy)—sitting all alone (you've been dying to meet this person). You make your way to the table (be sure you look all right—every hair in place . . .).

You approach and say something really really "cool" and ask to sit down. Your dream person says, "Sure." You pull out the chair, but suddenly your foot gets caught, and you trip, spilling your spaghetti, mystery meat, and drink all over her (or him). Angry, she (or he) yells at you and walks away. Everyone is looking and laughing. You try to hide as you clean up the mess.

■ **Shoppers' World**—It's the day after Thanksgiving, and you've decided to go Christmas shopping . . . on the busiest shopping day of the year. You drive around the lot looking for a parking place. Finally you spot one, and you race to beat the car coming from the other direction. You do, just barely, but the driver honks and shakes his fist at you.

Now you're inside, elbowing and shoving your way through the mass of humanity. There's Joan—you haven't seen her for months—wave—oops, you dropped the shirt—now look at it with a nice footprint on the collar.

Finally you're ready to get out of the mess. Your arms are piled high with gifts, carefully selected during the last couple of hours. You are in line at the counter, waiting to pay. The lady in front of you is taking forever, and the gifts are getting very heavy. Now it's your turn; one by one you give your purchases to the cashier, and she rings them up. You see the total bill—gasp! "Oh well," you think, "it's Christmas." You reach for your wallet—it's not there!

Note: **Imagination** may be done as a crowd-breaker or as a discussion starter. If you discuss it, ask if and why each situation represented failure; if they could identify with the situations; what other situations would have been good to act out; etc.

In the Cards ■ Give everyone a card (regular playing cards or some other kind with point values), and tell them to keep theirs a secret. Next, divide into two "teams" and have two members, one from each team, come to the front one at a time and expose their cards. Add up the totals for the teams and eliminate the team with the fewest points. Repeat the process with the "winning" team, dividing it into two halves, passing out the cards, and checking the totals. Continue the elimination process until you get down to one person—the champ!—and award a prize.

If you'd like to discuss this, ask:

- **How did you fell about losing?**
- **Did you feel like a failure?**
- **How does this experience parallel life?**

Numbers Victims ■ Choose a few audience reactions like laughter, applause, and cheering. After most of the kids arrive, practice these reactions and then assign each reaction a number. Explain that whenever you yell out a specific number, they should give the appropriate sound.

Keep a lookout for latecomers. Then, as they enter the room, give the crowd a number and let them react. The latecomer becomes an instant crowd-breaker "victim," thinking that he or she has just missed a great activity.

When you get to the discussion section of the meeting, refer to this activity and ask when in real life kids have felt excluded from certain activities.

Puzzled ■ Bring a few children's puzzles—make sure you have enough pieces so that everyone will have one piece. Place all the puzzle pieces in a bag and mix them up. To make it a little tougher, you may want to include one or two extra pieces that don't fit in anywhere.

Have each person draw out one puzzle piece and write his or her name on the back. Place the puzzle shells around the outside of the room. Explain that at your signal they should put their puzzle pieces where they belong; when they get them in place, they should sit down. Give a penalty for those who don't get the pieces in or who have them placed wrong.

Note: This also may be used as a discussion starter because it is symbolic of our experience of trying to find our places, where we fit into life. Some never quite make it. Others are rejected simply through "chance," not being given the natural characteristics and abilities.

Rats, I Missed! ■ This is a skit involving one person and a wastebasket. Introduce the actor as a great student who will be giving tips on studying. He (or she) then sits down in a chair (desk) with a stack of papers. About 10 feet away sits the wastebasket.

He then mentions that he is the world's greatest "crumpled-up-paper-into-the-basket-shooter." He just never misses! After crumpling up a piece of paper, he casually tosses it toward the basket and misses completely!

"Rats, I missed," he mutters, and then tries again. This continues for four or five shots with him missing every one and getting angrier and angrier while each time stating (and then yelling), "Rats, I missed." Finally he pulls out a gun and says, "That does it! If I don't make this next shot, I'm going to take this gun and shoot myself!" He tries, misses, yells, "That does it! Now I'm going to kill myself!" and stomps out of the room. The audience then hears two shots (use a cap pistol) and, after a short pause, "Rats, I missed!"

Right Moves ■ Explain that the theme of the meeting is *rejection,* a common experience. Then tell everyone to be seated and to move the direction you say if your description fits them. If someone is sitting on the place where they are to move, they should sit on that person's lap.

- Move 2 places to the right if you've ever lost an election.
- Move 3 places to the left if you've been turned down for a date in the last month.
- Move 1 place to the rear if you've ever been cut from a team.

- Groan if you've been turned down as a blood donor.
- Move 2 places forward if you've been ignored by a "friend."
- Move 1 place to the left if you tried out for a part in a play or a place on a squad and weren't chosen.
- Clap if you've ever failed a driver's test.
- Move 4 places to the right if you ever got fired.
- Sigh if you're afraid of not getting into the college of your choice.
- Move 2 places to the left if your teacher ever put you down in class.
- Move 1 place diagonally if you are not in the "in crowd."
- Turn around if you've ever felt like a "nerd."

DISCUSSION STARTERS

Charlie Brown ■ Choose a number of "Peanuts" cartoons where Charlie Brown is rejected. The Valentine's Day episode would be appropriate. Then ask when they have felt like Charlie, etc.

Ideals ■ Give each person an index card and a pencil. Have everyone write down the characteristics of the ideal person (certain to be successful) according to the standards of our society. One side of the card should be titled *Man* and the other side *Woman*. Collect the cards and compile two composite lists. They will look something like this:

Man

tall	wears the right clothes	good-looking
athletic or muscular	uses "Brut"	has money
owns sports car	outgoing personality	successful

Woman

blonde	dresses well	blue eyes
good figure	independent	owns car
outgoing personality	has career	has money

After the lists have been compiled, have all the girls stand, and then read off the characteristics, one by one, having them sit down when they don't measure up. Begin with the easier ones and move on. (E.g., "Our ideal woman has an outgoing personality; sit down if you're shy.") Continue until you have only one or two left and declare them "ideal women."

Repeat with the guys.

Discuss the experience. Ask:
- **How did you feel when you had to sit down?**
- **Was it fair to declare these people "ideal"? Why or why not?**
- **What's wrong with society's standards for acceptance and success?**
- **When have these standards made you feel rejected?**

Missing the Mark ■ Give everyone a chance to succeed at target-shooting with rounds of spitwads, rubber bands, rolled-up scratch paper, and other missiles. Point out that one definition of sin is "missing the mark." Discuss this definition and their experiences in light of Romans 3:23.

Nelson Nerd ■ Divide into groups and give the assignment of creating the typical "nerd," complete with name, personality, activities, and clothes. One team could have a guy play the part, and another a girl. When they're finished, the nerds should be introduced and say a few words about themselves. Then give each "nerd" a situation to improvise. Situations could include:

■ asking someone for a date
■ trying to be "cool" at a party
■ having a run-in with the school tough guy
■ answering a question in class

After the laughs, ask:

■ **Do you know anyone like these nerds?**
■ **How do you think they feel about continual rejection?**
■ **With which situations could you identify?**
■ **What could you do to help "nerds" feel accepted?**
■ **How would Jesus respond at your school to "nerds"? To the "in crowd"? To "superstars"? To "burn-outs"? To tough guys? To you?**

Rejection Slips ■ Distribute cards and pencils and have everyone record two experiences when they felt rejected. These answers should be anonymous. Collect the cards and read them aloud. Comment on the most common ones, the unique situations, etc., and ask:

■ **Why did the person feel rejected?**
■ **Were those feelings valid? (Was he or she really rejected or really a failure?)**
■ **Was what happened fair?**

Some Total! ■ As kids enter the room, send them, one by one, to a side room (or a corner) where you have a roll of adding machine tape and assorted felt-tip pens. They should write a summary of two or three experiences when they felt like failures (or more if you have a small group). No names should be used. As they write, the paper will become unrolled; after each person has finished, the paper should be rolled over what that person wrote.

Later in the meeting, bring out the roll, unroll it, read, and discuss what they've written on it. With each item or experience, decide whether it was really failure or just a problem of false expectations, misperceptions, or something out of their control. Using the adding machine tape demonstrates how these experiences can add up and make us feel like total failures. Cut out those genuine failure experiences, and then burn the others. Then discuss the actual failures, asking what can be learned from them, etc.

DISCUSSIONS

Discrimination ■ Explain that children can be cruel to each other—sometimes it's intentional, but often the games they play discriminate and hurt. Ask your students to recall some of their childhood games. Discuss how each one might foster feelings of rejection. Games mentioned could include Duck, Duck, Goose; Red Rover; King of the Hill; Mother, May I? and others.

Then ask about choosing sides for baseball, basketball, spelling bees, and other school games. Were they ever chosen last or near the last? How did that make them feel?

Discuss the "in crowd" and "out crowd" in high school, and ask:

- How do we reject others, in subtle or obvious ways?
- When have you felt rejected at school?
- How about in your dating experiences?
- When is rejection good?

Expectations ■ Ask:
1. Up to whose expectations are you trying to measure?
2. What do each of these groups of people expect?
   a. teachers
   b. friends
   c. parents
   d. society
   e. church
3. What does God expect of us?
4. How does He react to our failures?
5. How can and should we respond to this?

Failure Fear ■ Ask:
- Why do we fear failure?
- What's so bad about failure?
- How can failure hinder our future actions? (Make us unsure, afraid to take chances, etc.)
- Which failures are more devastating than others?
- What do we do to avoid feeling like failures? (Avoid risks, rationalize our failures, blame others, etc.)
- Which "failures" are beyond our control? (Those caused by certain external circumstances, by unchangeable physical traits, etc.)
- What good can come from failure? (Try harder, learn humility, develop other abilities to compensate, etc.)

Rejection Feelings ■ Use this outline as a wrap-up or discussion guide.
1. Feelings of rejection are common—we all have them at one time or another in our lives.
2. Often society's standards—for looks, abilities, possessions, etc.—cause us to feel rejected.
3. It is important to analyze how we handle rejection and our feelings.
   a. We may *feel* rejected when we haven't been rejected at all. We may just be insecure.
   b. We may feel rejected because we are put into situations with very limited options. In a tournament where there is only one winner, for example, the other contestants may feel like failures. Or in an election, the loser may feel rejected by the voters.
   c. Feeling rejected does not automatically mean that we are wrong. Our rejection may illustrate how inappropriate or even wrong someone else is. For example, there may be wrong values which are widely held—the values of an entire group can be way off base.
4. We can take steps to cope with rejection and feelings of failure.
   a. We can separate feelings of rejection from the reality of rejection. (Ask yourself, "What is really happening?")
   b. If we are feeling as though we really are being rejected, we should face the obvious question, "Why?" and we should consider that options may be limited, others may be wrong, circumstances may be wrong and unchangeable,

we may be rejected for good reasons.

    c. We should remember what rejection feels like and determine not to inflict those feelings on others.

Emphasize the importance of a healthy relationship with God, the reality of His acceptance of us, and the necessity to talk to God about our feelings (Philippians 4:4-7).

Challenge your students to reach out and to accept others with Christ's love (1 John 3:11).

Resolutions ■ Although not many people still make New Year's resolutions, ask how many have and what some of them were. Then ask:
- **Why don't people "resolve" anymore?**
- **When did you keep your resolutions?**
- **How does breaking the resolution(s) contribute to our feelings of failure?**
- **What is a better way to change?**

BIBLE STUDIES

First and Last ■ The thrust of this study is that God's idea of failure and success is the opposite of the world's. There are four parts, each of which centers on a specific value, uses the phrase "The last must be first and the first, last," and includes a challenge.

1. MARK 9:33-37
Read the passage aloud. Then ask:
- **What were the disciples discussing on their trip?** (Who was the greatest.)
- **What was the significance of Jesus's statements about children?** (See also 10:15.)
- **Jesus says that to be "first," a person must become the very "last, the servant of all"** (verse 35). **What do you think He meant? What does this have to do with children?**

Summary: The world says, "I am the greatest," and that successful people are confident and cool, full of *pretentions*. To be a follower of Christ, however, we must forget our image and become like children—open, vulnerable, with no hidden agenda, baring our deepest needs.

2. MARK 10:17-31
Have a volunteer read the passage aloud. Then ask:
- **What did the young man want from Jesus?** (Eternal life)
- **What did Jesus say the young man lacked?** (See verse 21.) **What happened?**
- **What did Jesus say that amazed the disciples?**
- **Jesus said, "But many who are first will be last, and the last, first"** (verse 31). **How does this apply to the situation?**

Summary: The world says, "Get what you can," and that success is measured by *power* and *possessions*. To be a follower of Christ, however, we must become poor—giving up, coming empty, with no hidden security.

3. LUKE 13:22-30
Have a student read the passage aloud, repeating verse 30 for emphasis. Then ask:

- **What picture or analogy did Jesus use to answer the question about how many will be saved?** (A narrow door)
- **What is the significance of the *narrow* door?** (You can only come by yourself, one person at a time, and you can't see what's on the other side.)
- **Jesus says, "Indeed there are those who are last who will be first, and first who will be last"** (verse 30). **How does this apply?**

Summary: The world says, "Surround yourself with friends," and that success is equated with *popularity*. So we surround ourselves with people who agree with us and reinforce our prejudices. To be a follower of Christ, however, we must come alone and in faith (not knowing what is on the other side of the door), willing to lose our friends and even our lives.

4. MATTHEW 20:1-16

Summarize the story and read verse 16 aloud. Then ask:
- **This is a difficult story to understand. What do you think it means?**
- **Do you think the owner was fair or not? Why were the workers upset?**
- **Jesus says, "So the last will be first, and the first will be last"** (verse 16). **What does this statement mean here?**

Summary: The world says, "Look out for number one," and that successful people have a right to be *proud.* So we want to work our way to heaven or to spiritual accomplishments and make sure that we get the credit. To be a follower of Christ, however, we must come with humility, thankful for His gift.

Summarize all four passages by saying: **Jesus turns the world's values upside down (really right side up). Real success is found in following Him as a child, poor, alone, and with humility. Real failure is failing to recognize and honor Him as Lord.**

Rejection and Christ ■ This Bible study has three parts.

1. Assign the following verses to students to be read aloud, one at a time.
   Luke 9:22
   Psalm 118:22
   Matthew 21:42
   Isaiah 53:3
   Luke 17:25
Then ask:
- **About whom are these verses speaking? How was Jesus rejected?**
- **Why would anyone reject the Lord?**
- **What does this tell us about rejection?**

2. Next, have these verses read aloud.
   Matthew 5:11-12
   Luke 10:16
   John 15:18-19
   1 Corinthians 1:23-25
Then ask:
- **How do these verses relate to the subject of rejection?**
- **When were you rejected because of your faith in Christ?**

3. Finally, have these verses read aloud.
   Hebrews 13:5-6

Psalm 139:7-12
Romans 8:35, 38-39

Then ask:

■ **What does God promise us?**

■ **How would these truths help us deal with rejection and our feelings?**

5

LONELINESS

A NOTE ON LONELINESS

"In the beginning" God pronounced that it was not good for man to be alone. We were created for relationships—literally we cannot live without others. Babies separated from their mothers and left alone suffer and die although their other needs are met; solitary confinement is an extreme punishment in prison. We need relationships with others. But there are two types of "others": God and people. The problem of loneliness cannot be solved unless both of these fellowship needs are met.

People are vital to us; we cannot live totally alone. The Bible is replete with guidelines, commands, and exhortations relative to our relationships—from the Ten Commandments to the Sermon on the Mount. Believers are instructed to love others and to gather in community for encouragement and worship.

The basis for loneliness is the absence of love, of significant persons who care for us. It is possible, therefore, to be lonely in a crowd, surrounded by strangers. Conversely, we may be cut off from everyone and not experience loneliness, knowing that there are loved ones who await our return.

Extended loneliness can be devastating. Psychiatrist Paul Tournier has said that loneliness is "the most devastating malady of this age" (*Escape from Loneliness,* Westminster Press, p. 8). It is a universal problem affecting every type of person. Loneliness may result from rejection by others, feelings of inadequacy, the loss of a loved one, a move to a new situation (home, job, school, etc.), or simply the overwhelming feeling that one carries a special burden that no one else really understands. By definition, loneliness is an intensely personal struggle.

But God can use these feelings to our advantage. Loneliness can help us take a close and honest look at ourselves, at others, and at God. In fact, many Christian leaders are encouraging us to break away from the noise and rush to an enforced "aloneness" and solitude, to meditate and listen to God. There certainly are precedents for this in the lives of Jesus, Paul, and others in Scripture.

Young people need to hear this message of encouragement and challenge. They should understand that:

■ they need friends and should develop close, honest relationships with peers, parents, and others.
■ God will never leave them. If they have a relationship with Him, they can talk to Him about anything, at any time.
■ loneliness can be transformed into a positive experience.
■ it is good to "get away from it all" and spend some time introspecting and communicating with God.
■ they should be sensitive to lonely people and reach out in love to them.

CROWD-BREAKERS

Belonging ■ Divide into circles of seven. Have each circle designate a person as #1. This game will proceed person-to-person clockwise around the circles. Here's how it works.
a. Person #1 turns to the person on the left, takes his or her hand, and says, "You are _____ (a one- or two-word compliment). I welcome you."
b. This person then turns to the next one to the left and says, "You are _____ (a different compliment). The one who is _____ (the compliment he or she received from #1) welcomes you."
c. This person (#3) repeats the process with the last phrase being "_____ (#1's description) and _____ (his or her own description given by #2) welcome you."
d. Continue around the circle with each person repeating all of the special descriptions of the preceeding people, in order, from memory (no helping), and their own.
e. Each descriptive phrase must be different from the ones used previously.
f. When there is a mistake made, the team must begin over. The first team to go around the circle first, wins.
g. For a second round, have them go the opposite direction, and go around twice. The last person will end up saying something like: "You are 'gregarious'! 'Beautiful,' 'warm smile,' 'nice hair,' 'good voice,' 'friendly,' 'loyal,' 'honest,' 'smart,' 'great eyes,' 'macho,' 'musical,' 'mellow,' and 'act together' welcome you."

Crowded Out ■ Mark a circle on the floor (with masking tape or string). It should be large enough for everyone to fit into it with about a foot to spare all the way around. Give everyone blindfolds and move them into the circle. Explain that when you blow the whistle, they should try to stay in the circle while pushing the others out. The only catch is that they may not use their hands. As each person crosses the edge of the circle, pull him or her to the side to observe the rest of the chaos. Continue until only one person (or a few) is left.

Freeze Dodgeball ■ If you have enough room, play a variation of the children's game "dodgeball." Two teams face off on opposite halves of a gym floor and take turns throwing soft, rubber balls at the legs of the opposition—no one may cross the center line to throw or to retrieve a ball. Those who are hit are "out."

With this version, instead of eliminating those who are hit, they must freeze in position. Each team, however, may also have a "melter." The melter can "unfreeze" a team member by touching him or her with a tap on the head from a special wand. Of course if a melter is hit, no one on that team can be unfrozen. A team loses when all of its members are frozen.

Hug ■ Give everyone a card on which you have written four numbers between 1 and 10. Tell them that you will be calling out two numbers at a time in each round. If they have one of the numbers you call, they should find a person with the other number and hug that person. (You can be sure that everyone gets a chance to hug if you include 1, 2, or 3 on every card and use one of those numbers in every call.) If a person's card contains both numbers called, that person must find someone with another called number and hug him or her. Eliminate the un-huggers and/or the last ones to get together, and continue until there are only a few left. Proclaim them the winners.

As a variation without cards, simply call out a number and have the crowd arrange themselves into group "hugs" of that number. The last group to form is eliminated.

Isolate ■ Have everyone stand. Then tell them to sit down when you read a sentence that applies to them. Continue this until only one person is standing. This will be fun, but it will also tell you something about the group and their "alone" experiences.

Sit down if . . .
■ **you've lost at "Solitaire."**
■ **you moved here within the past month.**
■ **you came home and found out your parents had moved.**
■ **you are an only child.**
■ **your best friend *did* tell you.**
■ **you are in a class where you are the only Christian.**
■ **you have been put down by friends for saying what you really thought.**
■ **you have been put down by a teacher for stating your beliefs.**
■ **you know someone who seems to be very lonely.**
■ **you recently felt like an outsider.**
■ **you feel funny right now, standing by yourself when everyone else is sitting down.**

Add others or create your own list and repeat the process. You can also use most of these statements as discussion starters.

Just Me ■ Before the meeting, cut out magazine pictures of a variety of products or items and tape each one to a piece of cardboard. Possible items could include hairspray, typewriter, dog, cat food, college, tree, hamburger, lake, Coke bottles, book, and so on. Be sure to prepare enough so that everyone will receive a picture.

Distribute pens and the pictures, instructing group members not to show them to anyone else. Have each person find a place away from everyone else where he or she can sit and write on the back of the picture why it is a symbol of his or her life. For example, a person with a picture of a dog could write: "This dog symbolizes me because I am a good friend. Usually my bark is worse than my bite."

After they have finished writing, have everyone turn in the pictures. Redistribute them, making sure that no one gets his or her own. Each person's task then is to try to match the picture with its owner. They should circulate throughout the room and may speak to only one person at a time, asking, "Is this the real you?" When a person makes a correct match, he or she should link arms with the person and together continue to search for the other one's picture-person. Chains of kids will be produced.

Note: This can be light or serious. Allow group members to write any descriptions of themselves that they wish.

44

Left Behind ■ Have everyone line up along one wall, shoulder to shoulder, with no second rows. Explain that you will read a description. If the description fits them, they should take one step forward. If not, they are eliminated from the game and must stand where they are until the game is over. Even if subsequent descriptions fit them, they may not move after they have been eliminated.

Draw a description out of a box and read it. Continue to read descriptions until a winner is determined (the last one left) or until the winners reach the opposite wall. Here are some possible descriptions:

■ You are wearing shoes with laces.
■ You are not wearing socks.
■ You brought a wallet to the meeting.
■ Your last name has three or more vowels in it.
■ You have a comb or a brush with you.
■ You live two miles or less from here.
■ You have never received a parking or traffic ticket.
■ The last five numbers in your phone number, when added together, total more than 20.
■ You have come to our last three meetings counting this one.

Afterward you may want to discuss how they felt being left behind, the "fairness" of the descriptions, and when they were eliminated by circumstances beyond their control.

Left Out ■ This works best with chairs but may also be done sitting on the floor in a tight circle. Arrange the chairs in a circle with everyone seated. There should be the same number of chairs as participants. Choose one person to be left out of the circle. This person vacates his or her chair and stands in the center. At your signal, he or she should try to regain a place in the circle by sitting in an empty chair. Everyone else, however, must fill any empty chair on their immediate right.

As the game proceeds, the left-out person is running clockwise around the circle trying to anticipate the vacancy and be seated, while the circle is moving counter-clockwise. When the left-out person is successful at claiming a chair, the person who allowed it (was not fast enough at filling the vacancy) must go to the middle.

Be careful, because this can get a little rowdy. To spice things up a bit, yell **Switch** to have them change directions. Later, add another person to the middle, vacating two chairs.

Let Us . . . ■ Give each person a leaf of lettuce with instructions to think of a pun using the word *lettuce* ("let us") and form a sculpture with the leaf to represent the pun. Here are some possibilities:

■ lettuce alone
■ lettuce pray
■ lettuce spray
■ lettuce leaf (leave)
■ he lettuce around
■ lettuce be free
■ lettuce see
■ lettuce run with patience
■ lettuce hold the lettuce
■ lettuce (lattice) work
■ lettuce entertain you
■ we were lettuce-tray (led astray)

After a few minutes, have the sculptures displayed and explained.

DISCUSSION STARTERS

Assignment ■ Distribute the following "Inventory" and have kids go off by themselves and take about 15 minutes to fill it in completely. After they return, discuss the process and their feelings, or discuss how God relates to their feelings about themselves, their personal goals, and their lonely times. Then spend time praying together for each other.

INVENTORY

The real me	What I want from life	Who I love & who loves me	How I see God in my life

Deserted ■ Divide into groups of seven and give each group a paper bag in which you have placed seven prepared cards. (The groups should have identical sets of cards.) Have each person draw one card and hold it quietly. Next, explain that each group has been stranded on an ocean island. There is one life raft with them, but it can hold only six people. Whoever stays behind is certain to die, but only six (maximum) can fit in the raft. They must decide as a group who stays and who escapes and survives. On each card write one of the following:
1. You are very strong.
2. You are very good-looking.
3. You are very wealthy.
4. You own the raft.
5. You are very intelligent.
6. You have a great personality and are well-liked.
7. You are a hard worker.

After a while, ask each group to report by answering these questions:
■ **How did you choose who would survive and who would be left behind?**
■ **If you were the one chosen to stay behind, how did you feel? Was the decision forced on you, or did you agree to it? Was it fair? Why or why not?**
■ **When do you feel "deserted" at school? Why are you left behind there?**

Drip Sculpture ■ Break into twos and give each pair a small candle, matches, and an index card. Tell them to light the candles and to drip the wax onto their cards to create a wax sculpture symbolizing loneliness. Allow a few minutes and then have the sculptures displayed and explained.

Note: When you do this, make sure to protect the furniture and the floor so that nothing is damaged by the fire or wax.

Isolated ■ Give each person a card and a pen. Have them sit as far apart as possible. Tell them that this is a "word association" game. That is, they should clear their minds and record the first word they think of after each word that you read aloud. Here are words to use in the association:

- movie
- date
- test
- face
- ten
- friend
- funny
- Selleck
- loner
- money
- dream
- reject
- happy
- vacation
- future
- alone
- one
- solo
- single
- couple
- solitude

Review each word and have them share their answers. There will be many humorous ones. Note especially the responses to *friend, loner, reject,* and *alone.* Discuss these or simply refer to them later in your wrap-up.

Loneliness Hot Line ■ Establish a "loneliness hot line," using your phone number and those of sponsors and kids who volunteer. Print these names and numbers on cards and distribute them to the group. Encourage group members to call whenever loneliness strikes and they need a person with whom to talk or pray.

Lonely at the Top ■ Hand out the following worksheets. Make sure to leave plenty of space for answers.

LONELY PEOPLE?

	Why is loneliness a part of this person's job?	What are the benefits of his/her loneliness?	What are the drawbacks of his/her loneliness?
Policeman			
Principal			
Parent			
President of U.S.			
Coach			
Class officer			
Cross-country runner			
Writer			

Discuss the answers, going through each category or through each occupation.

Lonely Times . . . ■ Distribute cards or half sheets of paper on which you have written the following incomplete sentences. Allow a few minutes for everyone to complete the sentences (they should not put their names on the papers). Collect them. Then take one sentence at a time, read the answers aloud, and discuss them.
1. Loneliness is . . .
2. The loneliest person I have ever known was (no names please) . . .
3. I feel lonely when . . .
4. The loneliest I've ever felt was when . . .

Many Faces of Loneliness ■ Using video equipment or a Polaroid camera, take pictures of everyone's posed loneliest face. This can be done during crowd-breakers, announcements, or discussions. Send each student individually into a separate room for the posing, and then tell them not to tell the others what they did when they go back to the group. After everyone has finished, display the pictures or play the video. It'll be a lot of laughs. Next, bring out a poster board on which you have taped (and numbered) a variety of pictures. (Note: Cut the pictures out of magazines and newspapers, and make sure that you have a variety of ages, races, and facial expressions represented.) Hand out pieces of paper and have everyone write down the numbers of the pictures of the people who they think are lonely. When everyone has finished, take a poll on the pictures, seeing how many chose each one. Ask them why they thought each pictured person was lonely. Be sure to make the point that *everyone* is a candidate for loneliness.

DISCUSSIONS

All the Lonely People ■ Discuss each of the following sources of loneliness. After describing each one, ask whether the kids know any people who fit that specific category—then have them share personal experiences.
1. **A poor view of self (results in separation from self)**—We fail to see how anyone could like us, and so we end up at home . . . all alone.
2. **Rejection by others—assumed or real (results in separation from others)**—We experience (or think we experience) put-downs, insults, and rejection from our peers, parents, or others, and so we withdraw, keeping to ourselves in our own private world.
3. **Loss (results in separation from others, or God if we blame Him)**—Tragedy, divorce, or another critical loss knocks us for a loop, and we don't know how to respond. Thinking that no one else understands or cares, we withdraw.
4. **Overwhelming personal struggles**—Similar to #3.
5. **Our sin (results in separation from God)**—Sin is everything we do which displeases God—ignoring Him, disobeying Him, putting ourselves before God and others. Sin causes guilt and results in alienation.

Alone: Happy or Bored? ■ Give the following suggestions for making the most of one's "alone times."
■ Learn something new.
■ Get some exercise.
■ Read.
■ Rearrange or redecorate your room.

- Help others.
- Explore and deepen your family relationships.
- Think and plan.
  Then ask:
- **When do you have a lot of time on your hands?**
- **How do these suggestions sound—how realistic are they?**
- **Have you ever tried them? Can you think of others?**
- **When do you have your "Quiet Time" alone with God?**

Alone Points ■ Use the following points as an outline for a wrap-up or a discussion.
1. Being alone can be an opportunity for us to look at who we really are, to see and appreciate our loved ones, and to move closer to God.
2. Often we are afraid to be alone—we can't even enter a room without turning on the television or radio. Maybe we don't like ourselves or don't want to have to think. But we need to be alone at times . . . to get away by ourselves to think, plan, and pray.
3. No matter how lonely we feel or wherever we are, we are never totally abandoned. God loves us and is with us.
4. Our world is filled with lonely people who need us, need our touch. We must reach out with the love of Christ.

Inside Loneliness ■ Use the opening statements for each point and then ask the questions printed afterward.
1. **Some think that one of the benefits of loneliness is that it pushes us toward ourselves. What do you think this means? Why would it be healthy to take a "self-inventory"?**
2. **Another stated benefit of loneliness is that it pushes us toward other people. How can this happen if a person is alone? What kind of risks are there when we open ourselves to others?**
3. **It has been said, "Loneliness hurts, but it also instructs." How does loneliness instruct? What does it teach us? When have you found this to be true?**
4. **Loneliness can also push us toward God. Do you believe this? Why and how would this happen?**

Lonely . . . or Just Alone? ■ Explain that there is a difference between being alone and being truly lonely (a person can be very lonely in a crowd). Discuss for a few minutes the advantages and disadvantages of being alone.
    Advantages: time to think, plan, create, rest, reflect, pray, etc.
    Disadvantages: feeling cut off, abandoned, unloved, deserted, friendless, etc.
    Then emphasize the fact that we are never totally alone—God is always with us. (Read appropriate verses like Romans 8:38-39.) Hand out papers and pens and ask each group member to write a brief poem describing either lonely feelings he or she has had or the profound truth that we are never separated from God and His love.

Other Lonely People ■ Ask:
- **Think of the lonely people in your life—at home, at school, on the job. Why are they lonely?**
- **How can you be part of the solution to their loneliness? Have you ever tried? What happened?**

■ **How would Jesus act toward these lonely people? What would He do?**

Sources of Loneliness ■ Use this as a wrap-up or a discussion guide.

1. **We can make ourselves lonely; it can come from the inside.** Loneliness from the inside can come from the fear of exposing the real us to the real world because of potential rejection or ridicule. So we hide who we are and outwardly become a clone of what society says is real. Left like this, we do everything we can to deal with that aching emptiness. Our only freedom will come from finding the security in ourselves which allows us to be ourselves in the world, with confidence, regardless of the world's reaction. This freedom comes from a solid relationship with God, who says that we are important just the way we are and that the real us is valuable. We are so valuable, in fact, that He sent Jesus, His only Son, to die for us. As we become open and real, some people will be attracted to that type of honest person, and deep relationships will be formed. But in the end, loneliness can be solved only by realizing that God will "never leave us or forsake us."

2. **Others can make us lonely; it can come from the outside.** Loneliness from the outside has many causes, but, more often than not, it results from not fitting into society's expectations. Some of the ways we fail to fit in are:
   ■ We aren't as attractive as society says we should be.
   ■ We aren't as physically capable as society says we should be.
   ■ We don't have the money or other things society says are important.

   The Bible tells us that Jesus often went to a lonely place to pray, to get direction from His Father, to confirm His course. We need to learn to use our alone times as Jesus did.

3. **Jesus can relate to our feelings of utter loneliness.** Jesus was in a world where even His closest followers could not understand what was going on inside Him, even when He tried to tell them. (We also experience loneliness when others cannot or at least don't attempt to understand what is going on inside us.) But at least Jesus had His Father.

   Jesus was alone in the garden when even His closest followers could not remain awake while He was so distraught He was sweating blood. But at least He had His Father.

   He was alone when He went through the mockery of a trial and when He was abused, marched up Calvary, and nailed to the cross. But at least He had His Father.

   When He hung on the cross and died, He experienced utter loneliness and rejection such as we have never known. At that point, He hung suspended between a world that had totally rejected Him and turned its back on Him, and His Father who also rejected Him. He became sin for us. In that instance, Jesus hung alone, utterly hated and rejected.

   We have a Lord who can relate to our feelings of loneliness, and who waits ready to meet our needs.

(Special thanks to Kevin Flannagan, Executive Director of East Alabama Area Youth For Christ, for this wrap-up.)

BIBLE STUDIES

Biblical Loneliness ■ Using leaders for each group, break into small groups and give each group one of the following sets of verses with discussion questions to look up and to discuss together. (Sample answers for your use are in parentheses.)

Then come back together as a large group and have the group leaders report the findings of their groups (in the order below). (Note: You can break the sections focusing on JESUS and on PROMISES into two groups each if you need more groups.)

■ JESUS
1. Read Matthew 26:36-46 and Luke 22:39-46.
2. What was Jesus feeling? (anguish, loneliness)
3. Why? (He had a burden to bear; He was facing the cross alone; all the disciples would leave Him.)
4. When was Jesus deliberately alone? (Matthew 4:1ff—temptation; Matthew 14:13—after the death of John the Baptist; Matthew 14:23—for prayer; Matthew 15:21, 29—new ministry)

■ JOHN THE BAPTIST
1. Read Matthew 11:1-15.
2. What was John experiencing? (doubt, loneliness)
3. Why? (He was imprisoned and cut off from Jesus and his other friends and loved ones.)
4. Why do doubt and loneliness go hand in hand?

■ PETER
1. Read Matthew 26:31-35, 69-75.
2. What was Peter feeling? (verse 75) (despair, shame, loneliness)
3. Why? (He had turned his back on His Lord; Jesus was going to be executed; all the disciples had fled.)
4. When was Peter's loneliness "cured"? (See John 21:15-19.)

■ US
1. Read Psalm 66:18; Proverbs 15:29; Ephesians 2:12; 4:17-19.
2. What do these verses tell us about a cause for loneliness? (separation from God)
3. What causes this problem? (self-centeredness, disobedience, lack of communication, etc.)
4. How is this problem solved? (See Colossians 1:20-21; 1 Peter 3:18; Romans 3:24; 5:1.)

■ PROMISES
1. Read Joshua 1:9; Psalm 23:4; Isaiah 49:14-15; Matthew 28:20; Romans 8:38-39; Philippians 4:19.
2. What promises do each of these passages give us? (He will be with us, never leave us, and meet all our needs, etc.)
3. How do these promises "cure" loneliness?
4. How should we react when we feel lonely?

Jesus and Loneliness ■ Have someone read Matthew 27:46 and Psalm 22:1 aloud. Then ask:
- **What was Jesus feeling?**
- **Why had God "forsaken" Him?**
- **How does this verse relate to Hebrews 4:15-16?** (Read aloud.)
  Next, have selected kids read the following passages.
1. Matthew 4:1

2. Matthew 14:22-23
3. Matthew 26:36-45
   After each one ask:
- **Why was Jesus alone?**
- **Was He lonely? Why or why not?**
- **What happened as a result of His aloneness?**

Never Alone ■ Have everyone look up Genesis 2:18. Read it aloud and ask:
- **How does this verse relate to being alone?**
- **What's the difference between being alone and being lonely?**
   Then turn to Romans 8:35-39. Read these verses aloud and then ask:
- **Are we ever really left totally alone, deserted?**
- **When have you felt as if you were?**
- **How would these verse have helped you with your feelings?**

Part of the Family ■ Use the following verses as evidence for what it means to be a member of God's family.
- John 3:6 talks about being born into the family of God.
- Ephesians 2:19-21 and 1 Peter 2:4-10 discuss the implications of being in God's family.
- 1 John 3:1-3 says we are children of God.
- Romans 8:14-17, Galatians 4:4-7, and Ephesians 1:5 explain that we are adopted.
   You may also want to discuss the implications of these truths for how we treat our earthly families and our brothers and sisters in the faith.

6

DEPRESSION AND SUICIDE

A NOTE ON DEPRESSION AND SUICIDE

Obviously these are not the usual "up" topics which will help draw kids to a meeting; depending on the kids in your group, you may not want to advertise the topic ahead of time. Instead, let everyone know that this will be a typical meeting which will feature fun activities and a serious discussion of a relevant topic. Depression and suicide, however, are important issues which need to be addressed. Teenagers are quite susceptible to depression with their volatile emotions, intense introspection, and need for peer approval. Teenage suicide has become a real problem (the second leading cause of death for high schoolers), and loneliness is epidemic. Because depression is such a common experience, don't be surprised if you get a lot of appointments for counseling.

It is also important to understand that, although these subjects are quite serious and should not be treated lightly, you can still have a good time in a meeting in which suicide is the topic. But you must exercise great care, especially if someone close to a group member has attempted or committed suicide recently.

CROWD-BREAKERS

Bottled-up Inside ■ Choose four or five guys to compete in a Coke-drinking contest. After they come to the front, explain that they can drink only the foam that rises after the bottle has been shaken. (Use 12- or 16-ounce bottles of warm Coke.) Repeat with girls.

As a variation, if you're outside, use the foam as a long-distance fire extinguisher or for target practice (also a contest).

This illustrates the way we feel inside (and how we can "blow up") when our feelings are all bottled-up.

Breaking Point ■ Hold a series of "consumer product tests" to see which products are stronger. Begin with tissue paper: have sets of kids hold individual sheets and place marbles in them, one at a time, until the tissues break. Repeat with tissues that have been dipped in water. Other products to test could include rubber bands (stretch them and see which one breaks first), balloons (blow them up slowly and evenly and see which one bursts first), paper bags, and trash bags. You could also do this as a competitive team event.

This illustrates how people often feel just before attempting suicide—at the breaking point.

End of Your Rope ■ This is a competitive event involving a "swinger" and an "eater." The swinger stands on a chair and is given a 10-foot piece of string with a donut tied to the end. This he or she swings in the direction of the eater, who is standing about six feet away with hands behind the back. The eater is allowed to take only one bite per swing and may not use his or her hands. The first team to eat the whole donut wins.

Going Crackers ■ Have a race to see which competitors can eat a stack of saltine crackers off a table without using their hands.

Hard to Hold—So Much to Carry ■ Divide into two or more teams, line the teams up in columns, and give each team 20 balloons. Next, have each team appoint a "holder," who goes to the other end of the room (at least 10 feet away from the team). At the signal, the first person takes a balloon, blows it up, ties it, and then runs it to the team's holder, who must hold it. The runner returns to the end of the line and the next person repeats the process, and so on until all the balloons are inflated and held by the holder (if one falls, the person may not return to the team until it is held). After all the balloons have been delivered and held, the holder must pop all the balloons *without help*. The first team finished wins.

This illustrates the frustration and futility of carrying and holding too much.

I Scream ■ This is a competitive event involving teams of two: a "feeder" and an "eater." At one end of the room, place bowls of ice cream (one bowl per team) with spoons. Explain that the goal of the game is for the feeder to feed all of the ice cream to the eater. Here are the rules:
a. The feeder will be blindfolded.
b. The eater must not use his or her hands.
c. The eater will communicate his or her location by screaming, but may not use words.
d. After each spoonful has been fed, the eater must move to a new location.

Proceed with the game, and be ready to move the eaters after each bite and to clean up quickly when ice cream is dropped.

This illustrates the desperation of some people and how difficult it can be to reach them and meet their needs.

It's a Bad Day . . . ■ Get into groups of three and distribute papers with the following incomplete sentences. Possible answers are in parentheses—don't reprint those. Encourage everyone to be creative in finishing the sentences.
■ You know it's a bad day when . . . (you forget that the Listerine isn't apple juice.)
■ You know it's a hard class when . . . (you can't help notice how much the teacher resembles Jabba the Hut.)
■ You know it's going to be a bad report card when . . . (an insurance agent calls to

say your dad wants you to get medical coverage.)
- You know it's a bad cafeteria meal when . . . (you are physically abused by the "mystery meat.")
- You know it's going to be a bad date when . . . (she opens the door and asks who you are.)

After a few minutes, collect the sheets and read them aloud.

Limbo ■ Hold a limbo contest. Two people hold a stick at waist height and the rest of the crowd goes under the stick, one at a time, on two feet, without touching the floor with any other part of their bodies. Then the stick is lowered. The idea is to see who can go the lowest without touching or falling.

This illustrates depression as the experience of being "very low."

Pit Race ■ Purchase a number of different fruits with pits and put them in bags according to the number of teams you expect to have. Divide into teams and explain that in this relay each team member will run to the bag, take out a piece of fruit, eat it as quickly as possible, and then spit the pit into a bucket a few feet away (if the pit misses the container, the person must retrieve the pit and throw it in). The first team finished wins. The fruits could include peaches, prunes, grapes, avocados, apricots, nectarines, mangos, etc.

This is symbolic of being "in the pits."

Reporter without a Story ■ This skit can be a light way to get into the topic of suicide—be sensitive with its use.

SCENE: a deserted bridge (a bench, row of chairs, or a table will do).
A solitary figure approaches the bridge and climbs on it. He speaks:

REPORTER: Woe is me! I am a reporter without a story. I have nothing to live for. I may as well jump and end it all! (He starts to jump, but suddenly someone behind him shouts out.)

LAWYER: Wait! Don't jump! (He climbs up on the bridge.) I'm a lawyer without a case. I also have nothing for which to live. I may as well end it all too. Let me jump with you. (Together they begin to jump when a voice behind them shouts.)

DOCTOR: Wait! Don't jump! (He climbs up on the bridge.) I'm a doctor who has lost his patients; I have nothing to live for. Let me jump with you.

(This continues for three more characters. They could include an accountant with a poor countenance, a tall jockey (speaking gruffly) with a little "hoarse," a pastor with a past, etc. Finally, they all decide to count to three and jump.)

ALL: One . . . two . . . three!" (They all jump except the reporter who rubs his hands together gleefully.)

REPORTER: Five people jump from bridge. Wow! What a story! (Exit.)

Singing the Blues ■ Play "blues" music as everyone comes in.

The Ups and Downs of Life ■ Have everyone sing the chorus of "Beautiful, Beautiful Brown Eyes." Then explain that the next time they sing it, you want them to change positions according to the following instructions: they should begin seated, and everytime they sing a word beginning with *B* they should change positions and continue singing in that position until the next *B* word.

The positions: lean to the left, lean to the right, stand up, sit down, and then repeat. (In other words, when they sing "Beautiful," they would lean to the left. For the next "beautiful," they would lean to the right. Then on "brown," they would stand and sing "brown eyes." For the next "B" word, "Beautiful," they would sit down. Then they would sing "beautiful" while leaning to the left and "brown eyes" while leaning to the right. They would stand on the next "Beautiful," sit on the next "beautiful," and lean to the left for "brown eyes . . . I'll never love." Then they would lean to the right and finish the song singing, "blue eyes again."

Go slowly the first time through. Then try it again a little faster. The third time, go very fast.

This illustrates the "ups and downs" of life.

What's the Use? ■ Display a variety of unusual items—kitchen utensils work well for this—and see who can guess what their real uses are. Then see if kids can create new uses for them.

Point out that many people ask this very question about their "meaningless" lives—"What's the use?"

DISCUSSION STARTERS

Affirmation Bags ■ Give every person five index cards, a pen, and a small paper bag. Tell them to write on each card something about which they are depressed or for which they need to be forgiven (one per card). These should include hurts of family, friends, neighbors, coworkers, or other troubling situations. After everyone has finished, have them put their names on the outside of their bags and then pass the bags around, person to person. Each time they receive a bag, they should drop one of their cards in it (none in their own bags).

After all the bags have been circulated and all the cards deposited, have everyone get up and move to a different place in the room. Then have them pass the bags around again. This time, however, they should take a card out and write on the back of it a statement of encouragement or forgiveness. This could be a Bible verse that relates to the specific issue on the card, a biblical principle or promise, or just some solid, Christian advice. (They should not have their own bags yet.)

After all of the cards have been covered, return the bags to their owners and have them read what has been written on the cards. Then have them share aloud some of the situations and the words of encouragement which are especially helpful or meaningful.

Anonymous ■ Hand out the following questionnaire. Encourage everyone to answer honestly. Make sure that they are anonymous.

ANONYMOUS

1. What is your major cause of depression?

2. Have you ever thought "casually" about suicide?   yes   no

3. Have you ever thought seriously about suicide?   yes   no

4. What gives your life meaning?

Collect the papers and briefly scan their answers. Then read aloud some of the answers to question #4 and discuss them together. Use the answers to the other questions to give you a feel as to where your group is.

I Give Up ■ Hand out sheets with the following case studies on them. Have students briefly outline an answer to this question for each one: **These people have decided to commit suicide. What would you say to talk them out of it?**

■ Alice—her parents divorced a few years ago, and now she lives with her mom who ignores her and her stepfather who beats her. It's just not worth it. Suicide seems to be the only way out.

■ John—he is deeply in love, but his girlfriend has just dumped him for his "best friend." Life's just not worth living without her.

■ Bill—all his life he's wanted to be a football star. He has just been cut from the team, and so his dreams are shattered. Why go on living?

■ Julie—she was just busted for possession and now must face her parents. They will be sorry and hurt. She has really messed up her life.

■ Suzie—she has high standards for her life—grades, career, boyfriend, athletics—but she just can't measure up. What's the use!

■ Ben—he's so lonely, with no friends. He may as well end it all—certainly no one would care . . . or miss him.

■ Jeff—there's just too much to cope with in life, all the hassles. He's tired of it all—tired of living.

Allow about five to seven minutes for students to jot down a few thoughts on each person. Then go through each one and discuss the answers. Afterward ask:

■ **What are other reasons people take their own lives?**
■ **Are there any valid reasons? Why or why not?**

Joni's Song ■ Briefly describe the situation of Joni Eareckson Tada (a quadriplegic because of a diving accident in her late teens). Then play the song "Joni's Song" from the album of the same name. Afterward ask:

■ What can Joni *not* do because of her accident? (Walk, ride horses or bikes, dance, run, swim, bathe herself, plant flowers, hug someone, jump, throw a ball, drive, pound a nail, swing a golf club, etc.)

■ Which of these activities do people really count on to give their lives meaning—for recreation, for employment, for relationships, for fun?

■ How would you feel if all of those were taken from you?

■ What gives Joni's life meaning and purpose?

Mime ■ Obtain the services of a mime or recruit an actor or two from the high school drama department to mime a few depressing experiences. After each one, ask the group to identify the experience, to explain why it would be depressing, and to share how they could tell that the person was depressed.

Situations ■ Read the following stories aloud. After each one, ask the students what they would say to these individuals to help them out of their depression.

1. Mary's parents have just gotten divorced, and neither one seems to want her. She loves her parents but feels somehow responsible for their problems. Lately she has been talking a lot about how there's not very much to live for.

2. John's girlfriend, Sue, just broke up with him, and he is devastated. All day he has been walking alone in the park. That's where you find him—sitting on a bench, crying.

3. Marianne's parents want her to get straight A's, and they really put the pressure on. Nothing she ever does seems to be good enough for them. Today she found out that she was turned down by the college that they wanted her to attend, and she doesn't know how to face them. "It might be better to get out of this whole thing called life," she mutters as she walks away.

4. Franklin really worked hard in the election for class treasurer, and everyone thought he would win. But he lost—by a landslide. He is really down.

DISCUSSIONS

Depression ■ Write the word *DEPRESSION* vertically on the board and use it as your discussion guide. Go through the letters one at a time and ask for possible causes of depression which begin with that letter. These could include:

D—distance (from a loved one), defeat, death, drugs, dirtiness, darkness, dead ends, doubt, disorder, delays

E—exit (of a loved one), exclusion (from a group)

P—pressure, pride hurt

R—rejection, rain

E—expectations, endings

S—standards, stress, substance abuse

S—shortfalls, self-centeredness, sickness

I—irritants, ideals, ignorance, insecurity, incompetence, incurable disease

O—old age, out of control, outside (feelings), obesity

N—neuroses, nit-picking, noise

Then, using the same letters, ask for solutions to depression. Here are some possible answers.

D—dreams, doing

E—excellence, eternity (seeing from God's point of view)

P—prayer, perspective, progress, promises, priorities

R—rewards, relationships, rest, recreation

E—excitement, excelling

S—stillness, sleep, shower

S—success, silliness, sports

I—interests, involvement

O—organization, options

N—nearness, niceness

Difficulties ▣ Divide into groups of four or five and have the members discuss and record their answers to the following questions:
1. What makes life difficult for high school students? (List as many as you can.)
2. What are the top three or four of these reasons?
   Bring everyone back together and discuss their answers briefly.

Fighting Depression ■ Ask:
■ What is depression?
■ When and why do people get depressed?
■ How does it feel?
■ What do you do to fight depression?

Suicide ■ Ask:
■ **How many of you have known someone who attempted or committed suicide?** (Have them raise their hands.)
■ **Why do people decide to take their own lives?**
■ **If you saw a stranger standing on a ledge, about to end it all by jumping, what would you say to convince her to live?**
■ **What can give our lives meaning and purpose?**

Warning Signs ■ Ask:
■ **What are some of the suicide warning signs—indications that kids are thinking about suicide?**
■ **Why would any young person want to take his or her life?**
■ **What could you say to help someone who you think may be considering suicide?**

BIBLE STUDIES

Care ■ Explain that suicide is the ultimate act of despair and that society is increasingly accepting suicide as an option. But it is not a solution. God created us to live useful and productive lives—to bring glory to Him. Suicide rejects God's plan and devalues human life. Then look up these verses together and discuss the possible motives for suicide mentioned.
■ Job 3:20-23 (life's weariness)
■ Ecclesiastes 2:17 (life's futility and hopelessness)
■ James 4:1-9 (anger and disappointment)
■ 2 Timothy 4:16 (loneliness)
■ Matthew 27:1-6 (guilt and sin)
Emphasize that if they ever consider suicide, they should remember that you care and God cares about them. Close with an extended time of silent prayer.

Emptiness ■ Hold a 10-week Bible study on the Book of Ecclesiastes, focusing on the emptiness of life from a secular, God-excluded point of view, and the real meaning and purpose in life with God at the center of our lives.

Halt ■ Have everyone turn to 1 Kings 18 and 19 (the story of Elijah's classic confrontation and the defeat of the prophets of Baal, and his postvictory depression). Have the kids follow as you summarize the story. Then ask what caused Elijah's depression.

After a few minutes of discussion, point out that all of us are candidates for depression. Then, using an Alcoholics Anonymous acronym, explain that depression will often strike when we **HALT** (are **H**ungry; **A**ngry; **L**onely; **T**ired).

Then wrap things up by using another acronym, **STEPS**. When we are depressed, we should **S**top; **T**hink; **E**valuate (ask: Why am I feeling this way? What is positive on which I can focus? What does God think about me? What has God done for me? With what other person can I share my feelings?); **P**lan some action (think through and plan specific steps to take—i.e., get some sleep, eat a good meal, talk to the person with whom you're angry, do something fun with a friend); **S**tart moving.

Promises ■ For a Bible study on hope, have everyone find the promises given by God to us in Scripture. Allow about five minutes for everyone to find one or two. Then have them share what they have found and list them on the board. These will emphasize God's love (1 John), His nearness (Romans 8:38-39), His power and sovereignty (Job), His perfect plan (Romans 8:28-30), and others.

7

EMOTIONS

CROWD-BREAKERS

A Moving Experience ■ Explain that because the topic is emotions, you want to do a little experiment to test the emotional makeup of the crowd. Tell them to do the specified action if the emotional experience applies to them. Everyone is part of the experiment the whole time; no one is eliminated. They must hold their poses until otherwise directed. Ask everyone to be seated, and give the following directions:

a. **Stand up if you yelled at someone in your family today.**
b. **Turn around 180 degrees if you were feeling depressed during the past seven days.**
c. **If you are in love, hug the person next to you (sitting or standing).**
d. **If your team recently won an exciting game, jump up and down three times.**
e. **Move seven feet to your right if you are afraid of flying.**
f. **If you've cried recently, cover your face with your hands.**
g. **If your feelings have been hurt in the last month, whimper softly.**
h. **Stick out your tongue if you feel "blah."**
i. **Open your eyes wide if you're afraid of the dark.**
j. **If you hate this game, scream and be seated.**

As the Stomach Churns ■ These short skits depict two ways to deal with emotions. You can present them back to back or at separate times in the meeting. Use the same situation in both scenes. The first time through, the characters respond very calmly, obviously denying their real feelings. The second time, they overact their emotional responses.

Characters: brother, sister, mother, father.

Brother enters the room (sister is sitting and knitting). The brother gets tangled in her knitting. The first time through, she responds calmly: "Oh, nuts. Now I guess I'll have to start over." The second time through she yells: "You clumsy idiot! Now I'll have to buy a sheep, sheer it, make yarn, and start completely over!"

Next, the sister informs her brother that his dog died that morning. The first time through he says quietly, "Oh, that's too bad. Well, I guess she had to go sometime." The second time through, he gives a loud gasp and then a prolonged cry of grief, breaking down, pounding the floor while exclaiming, "Why me!" and then accuses his sister of being insensitive.

The next part to this wonderful soap opera could have the mother coming in to find out what's going on.

Then, the father returns home from a month-long business trip. He announces that he has been transferred to Bush, Louisiana, and the family will have to move, etc.

The emotions denied and later expressed in an extreme form should be anger, grief, fear, love, surprise, and anxiety.

E-Motion ■ As background music, play "Feelings," "I Second That Emotion," or another song about emotions. Choose three or four contestants and explain that their task is to guess the emotion that the rest of the audience is acting out (or, to make it more difficult, have them shout out the emotion which is opposite of the one being acted). Explain further that they will stand in front, facing the crowd, while behind them an assistant will hold up a card with an emotion written on it. As soon as it is raised, the crowd should act and the contestants should guess. The person with the most correct answers wins. Use these emotions: joy, anxiety, dismay, jealousy, romance, fear, dislike, depression, anger, sadness, love, hate.

Emotional Events ■ Choose a number of contestants to compete in one or more of the following contests:
1. An onion-peeling contest. Use small onions and don't have them too close to the audience. The first person to peel the onion wins.
2. Laugher of the year. Contestants laugh and are rated on originality, sincerity, facial expressions, and musicality.
3. Best angry facial expression.
4. Keeping calm. A guy must be able to keep his cool while a good-looking girl runs her fingers through his hair and whispers sweet nothings in his ear.

Feelings (A Touching Scene) ■ Choose four or five "volunteers" (or team representatives) and seat them in front, facing the rest of the crowd. Explain that they will be blindfolded and handed various items which they should try to identify by touching (no smelling or tasting). The crowd may not give any help.

Pass the first item all the way down the line, and then have them guess out loud. Award points for each correct guess. (If your blindfolds can be removed and replaced easily, remove them after each item to allow the contestants to see the item.) To make the contest more difficult, or if contestants seem to be changing their ideas when they hear other guesses, give them different, but equally difficult, items each round.

Possible mystery items could include nutcracker, staple remover, protractor, golf shoe-cleat tightener, mango, Anthony silver dollar, back scratcher, Mardi Gras dubloon, plate of shaving cream, egg separator, etc.

Let It All Out ■ Use as many teams as you wish and give each team a tablet of paper and a pen. Explain that you have compiled a list of clichés about anger. One person at a time from each team should come to you to receive a cliché. Then they must return to their teams and *draw* a picture of it. The first team to guess the phrase wins that round, and the winner of the most rounds wins the game. There can be no talking by the drawer, and he or she must draw only pictures (no letters). Possible clichés to use include:

- hot head
- teed off
- burns me up
- blow up
- short fuse
- pet peeves
- flying off the handle
- blew his stack
- the last straw
- boiling point
- thin skinned

Mad Magazine ■ Type the angry phrases listed below (and others) on individual slips of paper. Make sure you have a slip of paper for everyone. Type duplicates if necessary.

Pass out the phrases. Then distribute old magazines, pieces of cardboard, scissors, and tape. Explain that each person should create a picture of his or her phrase using the pictures (no words) from the magazines. After they have finished, have them display their pictures while the rest of the group guesses the phrase.

- she flipped her wig
- she raised the roof
- he did a slow burn
- she looked daggers
- he was in a blind rage
- she threw a fit
- he blew his stack
- she went bananas
- she vents her spleen
- he was beside himself
- she jumped down his throat
- he gnashed his teeth
- he bit her head off
- he got his nose out of joint
- he flew off the handle
- he spit nails

Signs and Signals ■ This game is a form of charades. Divide into teams. Team members take turns pulling slips of paper on which a "sign" is written or drawn. The player acts out the sign so that his or her team can guess it. Each person is timed to see how long it takes the team to guess the correct sign. The team with the lowest total time wins. Here are some possible signs:

- Right turn only
- Stop
- Exit
- No U turn
- RR crossing
- Danger
- Yield
- No left turn
- Beware of dog
- Entrance
- Deer crossing
- Slippery when wet
- Watch for falling rocks
- Soft shoulder
- Caution
- Don't feed the bears
- Wet paint
- Sharp curve

This ties in with the idea that our emotions are warning signs, alerting us to things about ourselves.

The General Days of All My Children ■ This is a skit involving the following characters: Director (he or she opens the show for the audience, instructs the actors, and corrects their bad acting); Mother (hair in curlers, wearing an apron);

Father (wearing a coat, white shirt, and tie): Mother-in-law (guy dressed like a woman); Son; Daughter; Mailman (the last person to appear in each scene—carrying a mail bag, he always delivers a "special delivery letter" with a different message each time. These messages should be a surprise to the rest of the cast); Meter reader (who enters at a different time in each scene and simply announces that he or she is "here to read the meter").

SCRIPT
(Fill in the gaps yourself or with ad-libbing.)

The Director calls the cast together in front of the audience and explains that he or she has confidence in them because of their great talent and because they are professionals. He then has them take their places and calls for action.

Note: ALL OF THE LINES IN THIS SCENE SHOULD BE DEADPANNED, DELIVERED IN ALMOST A MONOTONE, DEVOID OF FEELING.

(Mother is at the stove. Father enters and sits in a chair.)

MOTHER: Hi, dear. How was your day?
FATHER: Fine . . . I got fired.
MOTHER: Oh. By the way, I had a little trouble with the car in the driveway.
FATHER: I noticed the garage missing. Say, what's for dinner?
MOTHER: Liver and peanut butter casserole.
FATHER: Let's see . . . that's the third time this week, isn't it?
MOTHER: Fourth. Oh, I forgot to tell you; Mother's here.
FATHER: Whose?
MOTHER: Mine—and here she comes now.
FATHER: What a surprise.

(Mother-in-law enters and speaks to Father.)

MOTHER-IN-LAW: Hello, Stupid.
FATHER: Hello, Mother. How long will you be staying with us?
MOTHER-IN-LAW: Three months. (To her daughter) I told you you should have married Frank. He's so handsome and is now a millionaire. But no, you had to throw your life away and marry this slob.

SON: (Enters and announces) I need the car for my date tonight.
FATHER: It's under the garage. By the way, your dog died in the accident.
DAUGHTER: (Enters and announces) I won't be here for dinner. I'm running off with Freddie to join the commune-cult in Columbia.

(Daughter and Son begin arguing; Mother and Father begin discussing; Mother-in-law mumbles to herself.)

Mailman enters with special delivery letter which Mother takes and reads aloud (informing them that their house is being forclosed or that Grandma is tied to the railroad tracks or that the high school has burned down, etc.)

At this point, the director storms in, calls the cast together, and berates them for their poor acting. After reminding them of a few of the tragic moments in the play, he tells them to do it over—with feeling!

This time through, the lines are essentially the same except that they should be delivered with great emotion—intensely overacted. The emotions displayed should include shock, anger, fear, grief, disgust, etc., and the actors should use very dramatic gestures and other body language.

After the special delivery letter has been read, the director again should charge onto the set and call the cast together. In this pep talk/lecture, he should explain that life isn't that tragic and that they should lighten up a bit. Then he should send them to their places, and they should repeat the scene. This time, however, the cast delivers all the lines (and reacts to them) with extreme humor and laughter. Finally, the special delivery letter is delivered—it contains their "pink slips" (they are fired). The director then should clear the set.

Ups and Downs of Life ■ Choose two of your best performers to act out the following script. They should overact the appropriate positive and negative emotions as they read their lines.

> BOB: Hey Bill, how's it going?
> BILL: Well, Bob, I'm not so sure—I had quite a day. First of all, I had a great night's sleep.
> BOB: Hey that's good!
> BILL: No, it's bad. I was supposed to get up early for an appointment, and I overslept.
> BOB: That's terrible!
> BILL: No, the person I was supposed to see forgot about our appointment—so now he owes me one.
> BOB: Hey, that's great!
> BILL: Not quite. In the rush to get there, I got in an accident.
> BOB: Oh, no! That's terrible.
> BILL: Well, it was her fault—now I can get a new car!
> BOB: Fantastic!
> BILL: Except for one thing. The girl who hit me is that blonde from chemistry that I've been trying to get a date with for a month. Now I feel really rotten.
> BOB: Oh, yeah, that's too bad.
> BILL: But she felt worse, and I think she might be willing to go out with me now.

Add your own extra lines.

What Am I Feeling? ■ Make a list of as many emotions or feelings as you can (at least 30). Randomly select sets of three (or five with a very small group) of these emotions and write them on self-adhesive labels. It's all right to repeat some of them.

As kids enter the room, put a label on each person's back, being careful that he or she doesn't see the what is written on it. After everyone has been labeled, explain that they are to circulate throughout the crowd, asking individuals, "What am I feeling?" The person asked then will act out one of the feelings on the "asker's" card. The asker then can have one guess, after which he or she will be told whether or not it is right. The goal is to figure out all the emotions written on one's card.

64

DISCUSSION STARTERS

A Bad Day When ■ Hand out sheets of paper and ask each person to give several different answers to this sentence: "You know it's going to be a bad day when. . . ." Here are some examples: ". . . you brush your teeth with Clearasil by mistake"; ". . . you wake up and discover your family has moved"; ". . . you learn that you studied the wrong chapters just as you walk into a big chemistry exam."

After a minute or two, collect the papers and read the answers. Don't worry if they are mostly light and humorous. There will be opportunity for more serious discussion later. The object of this is to get group interaction going. If there are serious answers, save them and read them last.

Assignment ■ Tell your group members to carry around a card for the next week. On it they should list the specific situations and the feelings they evoke when they arise. Each evening they should review the card for that day and talk to God about the situations and their responses.

Color Me . . . ■ Pass out cards or pieces of paper to everyone. Also make available a large box of crayons with extra amounts of the appropriate colors. Tell them that their assignment is to draw a picture, graph, diagram, or other symbol representing their lives from an emotional standpoint. That is, what they are really like on the inside. Tell them that the following colors represent specific emotions:
■ blue—sad
■ red—angry
■ green—jealous
■ silver—cool (unemotional)
■ pink—living (romantic)
■ gray—blah (depression)
■ yellow—happy (joyful)

Then have them get into groups of two or more and explain their symbols to each other. If that's too threatening, close this by taking a few moments for silent prayer. Ask each person to tell God about his or her drawing and ask His help in accepting and harnessing those emotions.

Diary ■ Suggest that your group members keep an "emotional diary" for a week, recording their feelings and the reasons for the feelings. After a week, they should meet with another person from the group, share their diaries, and pray for each other.

Feelings Gallery ■ Cut out pictures from magazines and newspapers which display a variety of emotions. (Use at least 10 pictures.) Post these around the room. Distribute paper and pencils and tell the group to check out the pictures as though they were "art critics." On their papers, they should record each picture's number and the emotion they think it is portraying.

After everyone has finished, pick up the pictures, hold them up one at a time, and invite "critiques." You may wish to discuss them briefly, especially when there is a wide disparity in the responses.

In the Mood ■ Give everyone a pencil and a piece of paper with these emotions listed. After each emotion, they should write a situation where they usually experience that specific emotion.
■ fear

- love
- sadness
- hate
- joy
- hurt
- bitterness

Collect the papers and read the answers, one emotion at a time (be sure to keep the papers anonymous). When you get to a situation with which a number of kids seem to identify, stop and ask:

1. Why is this such a (fearful) situation?
2. How do you act when you feel this way?
3. What effects do your actions have on you? On others?

Locate That Feeling ■ Read a list of locations and situations and ask the group what kinds of feelings each one evokes. If you get an unusual answer, probe further to discover why. Here are some possible locations. Add others.

- At the top of the Sears Tower, looking over the edge
- At an ocean beach, walking in the surf
- Alone in a dark, silent cave . . . you feel something on the back of your neck
- Jammed into a packed stadium for the Super Bowl
- Poised at the top of a Black Diamond ski run, ready to descend
- Alone in a large, beautiful cathedral
- Walking slowly through a park on a sunny, spring afternoon
- In a cemetery, standing by a friend's grave
- Looking through your family photo album

Picture This! ■ Select a number of pictures from magazines and newspapers, showing people in a wide range of emotional situations. Hold up one picture at a time and ask the group to shout out the emotion the picture expresses to them. List their responses. When you run out of pictures, ask if there are any other common emotions that you haven't shown. Add these to your list. Then go through the list again and discuss the following questions for as many of the emotions as you have time for:

1. What kind of situation or experience can set off this emotion?
2. How is _____ (the emotion) usually expressed?
3. How can a person respond constructively to _____ (the emotion) when it hits?

Then comment that our emotions not only affect how we relate to ourselves and to others, they also affect our attitudes toward God. Set the stage for honest discussion by sharing a time when your own emotions influenced your feelings toward God.

Poll ■ Hand out the following questionnaire. Give them a "feeling"—they should write it in the space that is most appropriate. Then give them a minute or two to fill in the last few lines. After everyone has finished, find out which feelings fell into which categories. Then invite volunteers to share what they wrote at the bottom.

WHAT DO YOU DO WITH A FEELING?

_____ Express it

_____ Keep it to myself

_____ Take it out on someone else

_____ Hide, cover it up

_____ Translate it into physical activity

_____ Suppress it

_____ Pretend it's not there

_____ Laugh about it

_____ I don't know what to do

_____ Other _____

Relate an experience that you had with emotions and what you did to deal with your

feelings: _____

_____

_____

Tools of Emotion ■ Read a number of emotions, one at a time, and ask what "tools" are commonly used to help express these feelings, and which ones they use. Here are some possibilities:
■ grief (tissue paper)
■ anger (paper and pen)
■ hate (fist)
■ fear (mask)
■ love (gift)
■ joy (music)

DISCUSSIONS

Common Emotions ■ Ask:
1. **What emotions are most common to you? When?**
2. **How do your mood changes affect you? Others?**
3. **How do you handle your emotions?**
4. **What would you like to change about the way your emotions and moods affect you?**

Dealing With Emotions ■ This can be a wrap-up or a discussion guide.
   Summarize what you've learned in your discussions about emotions; then remind the group that:
1. An emotion is a physical response to a thought.
2. Emotions are not wrong, they just *are.*
3. We should analyze our feelings to discover their cause—there's always something behind them.

4. We must learn to control, not stifle, our emotions:
   a. channeling them toward positive behavior
   b. minimizing the negative effects
   c. expressing them appropriately
5. Jesus said that we are to be *in* the world but not *of* the world (John 17:15-18). The world lives on and for feelings without controlling them. But we should be different (2 Corinthians 5:17), *and* our actions should express Christ's love (1 Corinthians 13; 1 John 3:17).

Handling Emotions ■ Use this as a guide for a wrap-up or discussion.

Two of the most important steps in handling emotions and not letting them control us are:
1. Acknowledging them, and
2. Expressing them in a positive manner.

We can acknowledge them by being honest with ourselves about our feelings. One very positive way of expressing them is to be open with others and with God about our feelings.

Importance of Feelings ■ Use this as a wrap-up or a discussion guide.
1. Our lives are full of feelings.
2. Our feelings and how we show them will determine the quality of our friendships.
3. We learn to know ourselves better as we share our feelings with other people. God created us as emotional beings able to feel deeply. These emotions touch all areas of our lives: home, neighborhood, school, friendships. Because God created us and declared His creation good, emotions, as such, certainly are not bad. Even "negative" emotions like hate, anger, and fear are not wrong in themselves. They are just there. Paul said, "Be angry and sin not" (Ephesians 4:26). Evidently what is really important is what we *do* with our feelings, how we respond. Anger can hurt and destroy, but it can also motivate and energize us to positive action. The same could be said for fear, hate, and even love.

   And then, of course, our feelings may be irrational. That is, they may result from misconceptions of persons, things, or situations. As we get in touch with our feelings, we can deal with them and deal with life.

   Remember that Jesus wants to be Lord of *all* of life, including our emotions and the source of our feelings . . . and how we act on them.

Remember ■ Use this as a wrap-up or a discussion guide.
1. Emotions are real, and they are part of your physical and psychological make-up. *Acknowledge them*—don't pretend that they do not exist. Don't repress or try to bury them. They affect you and others.
   ■ Recognize that sometimes they are related to your physical state.
   ■ Recognize that they are normal—you're not going crazy just because you experience mood changes.
2. Learn to express them in a positive manner. In some cases this means a simple exercise of your *will*. You're also a *volitional* creature. This simply means that you can control yourself. You can make choices and then follow through. Know your strengths and weaknesses—identify what causes your mood changes and what triggers your emotional responses.
   ■ Be honest and investigate; then learn to back off when you are approaching that point where you no longer are in control.
   ■ The most important way of handling emotions is being able to have someone with whom you can share honestly what's going on inside you.

3. Understand that although your emotions may change, God doesn't. He will be your friend, your companion, regardless of how you feel. He is someone to whom you can turn no matter how depressed, angry, happy, sad, frustrated, or pleased you feel. He will always be there.

Road Signs ■ Explain that emotions are like road signs because they give us directions. Then say:
1. **Share a specific situation when your feelings gave you a direction—what did they say to you?**
2. **How did you respond?**
3. **What happened if and when you ignored the signs?**
4. **What would be a Christian response to feelings of fear? Hatred? Grief?**

Unhealthy Approaches ■ Read the following unhealthy approaches to dealing with emotions, one at a time, and discuss.
1. *Denying our feelings*
   a. How do we deny our feelings?
   b. Why is this unhealthy?
2. *Hiding our feelings*
   a. Describe the last experience of hiding your feelings.
   b. How did you feel? Did it help the situation? Why or why not?
3. *Doing whatever our feelings tell us*
   a. What's so unhealthy about this approach? At least we're not denying or hiding our feelings . . . right?
   b. What kinds of actions do our emotions tell us to take?

BIBLE STUDIES

Characters ■ Have a Bible study of some emotional Bible characters. See how David, Job, Joseph, and others handled a range of feelings.

Emotional Implications ■ Divide into groups and give each group a piece of paper with these verses on it. They should discuss the "emotional implications" for the Christian for each passage. Then bring the group back together, report, and discuss their findings as a group.
■ Philippians 4:4-7
■ Ephesians 4:25-27
■ 1 John 4:18-21
■ Matthew 5:4
■ Matthew 5:22-24
■ Matthew 5:43-48
■ Luke 7:32, 19:41; John 11:35
■ Psalm 126:5-6
■ Amos 5:15; Romans 12:9

Search ■ Before the meeting, list from a concordance the passages that contain references to various emotions (e.g., love, hate, fear, joy, despair, anxious/anxiety, and others). Divide into small groups (3-5 in each) and give each group a list of passages and a Bible or two. Have them look up the verses and decide what the Bible teaches about that emotion—by example or direct statement—and how and when it can be displayed.

8

FAITH AND DOUBTS

CROWD-BREAKERS

Blind Boats ■ Seat the group and divide into two teams by drawing an imaginary line down the middle of them. Explain that you are going to see which team is the most coordinated—able to think and act while they sing. Then have everyone sing together the old song "Row, Row, Row Your Boat." Explain that you want them to sing it again, but this time, they will have to change positions whenever they sing a word which contains the letter *r*. The team on your right should begin seated, and the team on your left should begin standing. When they come to an "r-word," whoever is standing should sit down (until the next r-word), and whoever is seated should stand up. They would change positions on these words: *row, your, stream, merrily,* and *dream.* Go slowly at first, until everyone can do it. Then sing it again, faster. Repeat the process with "Three Blind Mice." The r-words in this song are *three, run, ran, after, farmer's, their, carving, ever,* and *your.* You could also repeat the songs using the letter *l.* If they get too tired of standing and sitting, have them raise and lower their hands instead.

This game illustrates submission—by following your directions, they are submitting their wills to yours.

Doubts ■ Choose an unusual word from the dictionary (e.g., *laburnum, moquette, stertorous*). State the word and have group members write their own definitions on index cards. (Definitions may be serious or humorous, but they should sound official). Collect the definitions and read them to the group, including the correct one, which you have written on a card. Vote on the definitions and give points to each person according to how many votes his or her definition received. Repeat with other words or with Biblical characters.

This game illustrates how easy it is to doubt when people make contradictory claims.

Finish the Course ■ Using two teams, have each one choose a person to compete. Explain that these contestants will be blindfolded, brought into the room one at a time, and placed at a starting line. When you give the signal, another person from the contestant's team will shout instructions on how and where to walk. The goal is to navigate a specific course as quickly as possible without going off the course.

Have the contestants taken from the room, and set up the course on the floor. Use children's blocks to form the borders of a path about 18 inches wide. Put two turns in the path. Explain that for every block moved, 10 seconds will be added to the contestant's time.

Then bring in the first blindfolded contestant, place him or her at the starting line, and begin. Have everyone except the contestant and the instruction-giver seated, and make sure that the other team doesn't cheat by interfering physically or verbally. Also, appoint a staff person or two to be timekeeper and judge. After team #1 has finished the course, bring in the contestant from team #2. Repeat the process as often as you wish, but be sure to take the two new contestants out of the room while you design a new course.

This illustrates the importance of obedience. To be successful, the contestant has to listen, trust, and obey every command from his or her instructor.

Here's the Pitch ■ Divide into teams with four or five kids in each, and give each team a very unusual product. Try to find products that they haven't seen before—a computer part, a unique kitchen utensil, a carpenter's or plumber's tool, etc. The idea is for each team to think up a great sales pitch for their product. They should use their imaginations and creativity, emphasizing the fantastic properties and multitude of uses. Give them about five minutes to create, and then have the teams present their sales pitches and products. Encourage them to use all their team members in their ads.

The fantastic claims in this game illustrate the way we have become used to things which sound too good to be true and which later turn out not to be true—ads on TV, etc. As a result, we tend to doubt the latest set of claims.

I Doubt It ■ Give each person a piece of paper, a pen, and a safety pin (or masking tape). Tell them to write two statements on their papers, both describing unusual facts about themselves or events in their lives. One statement should be true and the other one false. They should leave about 1 1/2 inches of space on the paper under each statement. (Samples: 1. "I used to have a pet monkey named 'Ronald Reagan.' " 2. "When I was a baby, I had brain surgery.")

Allow a few minutes for them to think and write, then have them pin their papers to their backs. Explain that everyone should walk around the room and read the statements on each person's back. Then the reader should put a check under the one that he or she believes to be true (only one check per person, per back). Players should not tell anyone how they voted.

After everyone has voted on every person's statements, have everyone remove the sheets and sit down. Find out who had the most votes for a false statement (have a few of the top vote-getters read), who had the least votes for a true statement (have a few of the more unusual ones read), and who fooled the fewest people.

I Wonder ■ The goal of this quiz is to create doubt by the use of trick questions. The correct answers are in parentheses. Copy the quiz without the answers. Distribute it with pencils and allow about three minutes for students to complete it.

1. How many of each animal did Moses put in the ark? (None—it was Noah.)
2. How many dead soldiers are buried in the Arlington National Cemetery? (All of them.)
3. If "North" on a map is up, which direction is to your left? (It depends which way you're facing.)
4. Which of these insects is feared most by women: beetles, spiders, or butterflies? (Beetles or butterflies—spiders aren't insects.)
5. True or False—In the Bible, God turned stones into bread. (False; Satan tempted Jesus to do this, but Jesus refused.)
6. Do they have a fourth of July in Canada? (Yes, but it is not a holiday.)
7. If I have two coins in my hand totaling 55 cents (U.S.), and one is not a nickel, what is the other coin? (A nickel.)
8. Write the word that is the opposite of "up." (If "down" was *printed,* the answer is wrong—it was supposed to be *written.*)
9. What gets wet as it dries? (A towel.)
10. Without asking his or her name, who is the person sitting directly in front of you? (This is not a trick question, but by this time, they probably will think it is as you give the other answers.)

If you discuss this later, ask:
- **How did you like our quiz?**
- **What were you thinking as you answered the questions?**
- **When did you start looking for the trick questions?**
- **How does this experience relate to "doubt"?**

Magic Tricks ■ To illustrate that much of Satan's work involves deception and makes us doubt our faith, perform a few simple "magic" tricks. Here's one.

Before the meeting, tear a very small piece (about ½ inch in diameter) out of a newspaper, memorize the letters on it, fold it three or four times, and put it into your pocket. During the meeting, announce that you will perform an amazing mind-reading trick.

Bring out a newspaper and hand it to a group member. Have him or her choose a section. Then take that section and hand it to another student, who should choose a page. Take the page from that person and give it to another one. (Note: It is important that you take the newspaper from each student before giving it to someone else.) Have this person tear the page in half; take one half and give it to someone else.

Continue this process until the newspaper piece is about six inches to a foot square. Then hand this piece to a student and ask him or her to tear a small piece out of the center of it, about ½ inch in diameter, and to fold it three or four times. While he or she is doing this, slip your hand into your pocket and take out the piece of paper which you had placed there earlier. Take the small piece from the student, switch it with your piece, and hand yours (which everyone thinks is the one that they have just seen torn from the newspaper) to another person. Next, tell that person to hold the piece of paper in his or her right fist and to press it against his or her forehead.

Write on a concealed chalkboard or poster board the words on the paper which you had memorized earlier. Tell the audience that you are "getting the vibes," etc. Make sure that they cannot see what letters you are writing. Then have the person holding the piece of paper come to the front of the room and write on another board the letters that he or she sees on the paper. Afterward, turn around the board on which you had written, compare the answers, and watch their faces drop in amazement.

The Search ■ Before the meeting, scatter various items throughout the room. These could include rubber bands, paper clips, balloons, index cards, a tennis ball or two, a few colorful ribbons, a paper cup, and others. Explain that you are going to have an indoor scavenger hunt. But this "hunt" will differ in two ways from all the others which they have experienced. First of all, you will be calling out the items one at a time, and second, the hunt will take place in the dark.

Tell everyone to get ready and to be quiet. Then turn off the lights. (Note: This will be a lot of fun, but it will also be quite rowdy. Be sure that all the breakables have been removed, have everyone remove their shoes, and use a whistle to get their attention between items.)

There are no teams; it is every person for him- or herself. Yell out the items, one at a time, pausing between each one for a few seconds for the kids to search for it. Also, ask for one item that isn't in the room. After calling for 10 items, turn on the lights and see who has collected the most. For control purposes, during the game you may want to turn the lights on and off quickly to see how they're doing.

The tie-in is that when we have been in darkness for a while, we begin to doubt what we saw in the light. We're not really sure that those things are really there. Of course there are many kinds of darkness—sorrow, separation, lack of communication, and others.

Why? ■ Hand out the following quiz. Each answer begins with the sound "why." The answers are in parentheses.

WHY

a drink	(wine)
a high-pitched, irritating sound	(whine)
without color, bleached out	(white)
cunning	(wile)
out of control	(wild)
spouse	(wife)
extensively	(widely)
dispersed	(widespread)
meantime	(while)
waves	(whitecaps)
alert	(wide awake)
twist around	(wind)

metal strand	(wire)
lean, supple	(wiry)
learned, intelligent	(wise)
world famous beach	(Waikiki)
witticism, joke	(wisecrack)

DISCUSSION STARTERS

Announcements ■ Before the meeting, prearrange a "doubter" who will ask a number of good, legitimate questions about each of your announcements. Make sure that during the meeting you pause for about three announcements about upcoming events. During each announcement, allow time for questions, and be sure to try to answer your doubter. Later in the meeting, discuss the experience. Ask:
- **What did you think about the questions during the announcements?**
- **Is it good to ask questions? Why or why not?**
- **How does asking questions relate to doubting?**

Encouragement ■ Select a couple of sharp guys and teach them to do a specific crowd-breaker or a simple task. Time them to see how fast they can do the task. Have them taken from the room and bring them in one at a time and repeat the task. Have the crowd encourage the first one and discourage the second one (set up the crowd while the competitors are out of the room). Then discuss the effects of encouragement vs. discouragement; when they have allowed doubts and discouragement to affect their lives; how they can encourage others; how they can overcome doubt and discouragement; etc.

Roles ■ Divide into pairs to do the following role plays. Encourage the actors to play their parts as realistically as possible.
1. A is the parent and B is the seven-year-old child. A has promised to do something very special with B this weekend (and B has really looked forward to it for weeks), but something has come up and A can't go. A is explaining this to B.
2. A and B are best friends. A couple of weeks ago, A gave B a prized possession to use. Now B is explaining how he or she broke it.
3. B is the chairperson of the program committee and has given A a very important responsibility for the upcoming event. (A almost begged for the assignment.) Well, the big day is almost here and B discovers that A hasn't even started the assignment. What is really bad is that A had assured B that things were under control. (This has happened before.) B confronts A.

Pick up the discussion immediately following the role plays. Ask:
- **What kind of conversation did you have in situation number one? (What was the special activity? How did B feel? What was said?) Has this ever happened to you? How did you feel?**
- **In situation number two, A, how did you react to B's news? Did you blast, forgive, or gloss over? What will you do the next time B wants to borrow something? Why?**

74

- In our last situation, how did you both react? What excuses did A give? When has someone in real life (don't mention any names) let you down like that? What did you do?
- How do our role plays relate to the subject of doubt? What other circumstances breed doubt? How do our other games illustrate causes of doubt?
- How can these causes of doubt affect our faith in Christ?

Show Me the Way ■ Choose four volunteers to participate in a contest to see who can best follow directions. Blindfold them and line them up next to each other in front of the room. Explain that you will be giving them instructions on where to go. Without asking any questions and with no help from the audience, they should do what you say as quickly as possible. If they follow your directions correctly, they will come to a prearranged spot in the room. The person closest to that spot will receive the prize.

Read aloud the following instructions. Note that they are somewhat ambiguous or that the action taken will vary depending on the person. Add other instructions to fit your location and marked spot on the floor.
- Take five small steps forward.
- Turn right and take one giant step.
- Turn 20 degrees to the left and walk heel-to-toe for three seconds.
- Face north.
- Get on all fours and crawl for 10 feet.
- Turn around and go backward a little.
- Pivot 1½ times around and hop once straight ahead.
- Shuffle sideways three steps.

Afterward, discuss why these instructions were difficult to follow, how they are similar to those we receive from parents, teachers, pastors, and others about life, and when they feel like the blindfolded contestants. Then ask how your instructions compare to God's directions.

Survey ■ Three or four weeks before the meeting, survey the kids about the part that doubt plays in their lives—what or who is easy for them to doubt and why; what makes them feel doubtful about themselves; etc. Then in the meeting, discuss their answers.

Teamwork? ■ Before the meeting, copy the following set of instructions for each group member.
- Performer—Acting as the team representative, this person must complete a task as quickly as possible.
- Coach—While the performer is completing his or her task, this person should be shouting instructions.
- Cheerleader—This person should yell encouragement to the performer as he or she works.
- Doubter—This person's role is to question the rules, ask about the time and procedure, and point out the problems in the performer's work.

Divide into teams of four and distribute the instruction sheets. (Each team should have one person for each role.) Explain to the whole group that you will be having a contest of skill and dexterity. Each team will have the chance to compete against the clock. The fastest team will get a prize, and the losing competitor (the performer for the slowest team) will get a shaving-cream pie in the face. Any team not following the rules will be disqualified and lose automatically. NOTE: During this game, only the coaches can remind anyone else of the rules.

Demonstrate the task, and then begin the contest. Possible tasks could include assembling a child's puzzle, putting the pieces in the "Shape-o" Tupperware toy, working the children's toy "Perfection," stacking odd-sized objects, and others. Be sure to watch the actions and effects of the doubters.

After the contest, declare the winning team and award the prizes and penalty. You can discuss the experience right away or wait until later in the meeting. Ask:
- **How did you doubters feel as you played your roles?**
- **Was it difficult or easy to do? Why?**
- **You performers, how did the other team members affect your performance?**

Trust List ■ Write the following occupations on the chalkboard or a poster. Then give everyone a piece of paper and have them list the occupations in order of trustworthiness. Afterward, total the group's ratings. Ask why they think of a particular occupation or person as trustworthy or untrustworthy. Then ask what builds trust.

- politician
- store clerk
- medical doctor
- psychiatrist/counselor
- teacher
- police officer
- insurance salesperson
- minister
- car salesperson
- company president
- store manager
- pro athlete
- door-to-door salesman
- fire fighter
- writer
- waitress
- lawyer
- movie star
- rock star
- reporter

Yield ■ This game illustrates what it means to yield to another person's control. Afterward, discuss whether or not it is a good illustration of how we should depend on God.

Choose two couples to compete and bring them to the front of the room. Blindfold one member of each couple and give him or her a piece of chalk. Explain that you will give the other member of each couple a message on a card which he or she must print on the blackboard (or a large piece of paper) so that the rest of the group can read it. The catch, however, is that this person may use only the blindfolded person's hand to write the message. There can be no talking by the couples during the contest. The person who can see must hold his or her partner's hand and guide it on the blackboard. The first couple to finish the message so that everyone can read it wins. Repeat this with other couples if you have time. Use the following messages or create your own.
- Thanks for the help.
- Work through me.
- I am depending on you.
- What do you think this says?
- Now this is what I call creative writing.
- I really appreciate what you're doing for me!

Afterward, ask the blindfolded people how they felt about the experience. When did they use their own muscles? How did they decide to grip the chalk? Did they ever know what letters or words they were writing? Ask the seeing partners about the experience. When did it become easy to write the letters and words? How could your partner have helped you more? How would having the blindfolds removed have helped? How would talking to each other while still blindfolded have helped?

DISCUSSIONS

Antidotes ■ Outlined briefly are three antidotes to the main causes of doubt. Use this as a guide for a discussion or for a wrap-up. Be sure to illustrate with personal examples.

1. An inspiring Christian, Dr. V. Raymond Edman, often said in chapel addresses at Wheaton College, "Never doubt in darkness what God has shown you in the light." The only sure cure for darkness-induced doubt is to remember the light and what you experienced there. In other words, we can remember what God has done for us in the past. A personal diary or quiet-time log would be helpful to review. In the Old Testament, when Israel was traveling from Egypt to the Promised Land, they had to be reminded continually of God's faithfulness in the past and of His promise of protection and care. (See Deuteronomy 1.)

2. Jesus is the truth, and the Bible is the infallible Word of God. (Read John 14:6 and 2 Timothy 3:16-17 aloud.) Don't be discouraged or fooled by the outrageous claims you hear; instead, immerse yourself in God's truth. This is the cure for doubt caused by our society.

3. Human beings are fallible. The fact is that if you keep your eyes on humans, they will eventually let you down—no one's perfect. (Refer to the role plays in **Roles** if you used that discussion starter.) Even your leaders will sin; and if your faith depends on them, you will be crushed. Instead, we must keep our eyes on Christ. He is perfect, and He will never let us down. Look at Peter. He wanted to walk on the water like Jesus, and he did; but when he took his eyes off Christ and looked instead at his circumstances, he began to sink (Matthew 14:22-31). We must keep our eyes on Christ.

Good or Bad? ■ Ask:

■ **When is doubting good?** (When it stops us from being taken in by something or someone false, etc.)

■ **When is doubting bad?** (When it undermines our confidence in something or someone good; when it stops us from good actions; etc.)

■ **Is doubting a sin?** (Not automatically; it is what you do with your doubts that counts. There are times, however, when doubting is wrong in itself—when God has definitely told us to do or not to do something, etc.)

Prayer ■ Close the meeting with prayer circles. Have kids pray for each other and the situations which cause us to doubt.

BIBLE STUDIES

Belief and Unbelief ■ Divide into groups and give each group a passage and questions to discuss. After a few minutes, gather everyone together again and find out what they discovered.

1. Matthew 13:53-58
   ■ Who are the people in the story?
   ■ What did Jesus do for them?
   ■ How did they respond?
   ■ Why didn't they believe in Him?

2. Acts 17:18-34
   ■ To whom was Paul speaking?
   ■ How did most of them respond to his message? Why?

- How did those in verse 34 respond?
- What made the difference in the responses?
3. Acts 26:1-32 (especially verses 28-32)
    - Summarize the Gospel as presented by Paul in this chapter.
    - How did Festus respond? Why?
    - How did Agrippa respond? Why?
    - What would it have taken to overcome their doubts?
4. Mark 9:14-29
    - Summarize the story: what happened and where?
    - Why weren't the disciples effective?
    - Explain verse 23.
    - What did the father mean by his reply to Jesus? (verse 24) How does his response relate to doubting and doubts?

Seeking and Finding ■ Ask volunteers to look up the following passages and read them aloud, one at a time. After each one, comment on what the passage is teaching about doubt and faith.
1. **Matthew 11:1-6**—Even spiritual giants like John the Baptist had doubts when faced with incredible problems. When his questions were answered (and notice that Jesus took time to answer them), his doubts were relieved, and he believed.
2. **Matthew 13:53-58**—Some people refuse to believe, even when confronted with the facts. These folks are blinded by their doubts.
3. **Matthew 7:7-8**—It is good to ask questions if we are truly "seeking." Jesus promises that those who seek will find Him.
4. **John 20:24-31**—Thomas doubted, but Jesus didn't condemn him, because Thomas believed when he was confronted with the truth. The Bible is God's Word and was written to give us answers to our honest questions. We shouldn't be afraid to ask.
5. **James 1:5-8**—A "double-minded" person is someone who continues to slip into doubt, forgetting the truth of God's Word and the proof of his own experiences. We should not wallow in our doubts.
6. **Hebrews 11:6**—God will reveal Himself to those who honestly and diligently seek Him.

Close by reminding your students that doubt is natural and even healthy at times. Doubting can keep us from being taken by con men and can help us find the truth. Also, assure them that it is OK to doubt their faith—they shouldn't accept something as truth just because someone (even you) said it. They should search the Bible for themselves. But this questioning and searching must be honest, looking for answers. Challenge them to talk honestly to God about their doubts and encourage them to set up appointments with you to discuss any nagging doubts that they have—you can look for the answers together.

9

PRAYER AND PRAISE

CROWD-BREAKERS

Addresses ■ Pass out the following quiz. Have everyone fill in the missing parts of these famous addresses. (Answers are in parentheses.)

ADDRESSES

1. _____ Sunset Strip (77)

2. No. 10 _____ (Downing Street)

3. _____00 Pennsylvania Avenue (16)

4. _____ & Vine (Hollywood)

5. S_____ Street (Sesame)

6. Saks _____ Avenue (5th)

7. _____ S_____ and _____ years ("4 score & 7 years ago")

8. North _____ 40 (Dallas)

9. Elvis lived at _____ (Graceland in Memphis)

Mix in a couple of addresses of group members, the church, and your own. You can move from this activity into a meeting on prayer and praise by asking how we address our communication to God.

Blessings Galore ■ Divide into teams of 10 to 15 in each (with smaller teams, have them go through the whole team more than once) and have the teams stand in parallel lines. The first person in each team begins by saying, "I thank God for _____" (a blessing). Then the next person must repeat what the first person said and add another blessing. The third person repeats what was said by the first two and adds another one. For example, he or she could say, "I thank God for good health, great parents, and my dog." The process continues until the last person on the team repeats all the blessings with no help from other team members. The first team to get through the whole team wins that round. For round two, have the teams start at the other end and see how far they can get within a certain time limit. If they get through the entire team once, they should keep the process going by starting with person number one again.

Creative Communication ■ The following summaries have been circulated widely and are said to have appeared on accident report forms sent to a state office of motor vehicles. These drivers were trying to explain their accidents and justify themselves.

Before the meeting cut the excuses out and distribute them to group members, explaining that you will ask them to read the phrases later. Between each activity, have a few read.

These literary "classics" are excellent examples of poor communication. What was meant was not said. After each one, have the group try to figure out what really happened. This activity can tie in with communicating with God in prayer and praise.

1. A pedestrian hit me and went under my car.
2. A truck backed through my windshield into my wife's face.
3. I thought my window was down, but I found out it was up when I put my head through it.
4. The other car collided with mine without giving warning of its intentions.
5. The guy was all over the road. I had to swerve a number of times before I hit him.
6. In an attempt to kill a fly, I drove into a telephone post.
7. I collided with a stationary truck coming the other way.
8. Coming home, I drove into the wrong house and collided with a tree I don't have.
9. To avoid hitting the bumper of the car in front, I struck a pedestrian.
10. The pedestrian had no idea of which direction to run, so I ran over him.
11. An invisible car came out of nowhere, struck my car, and vanished.
12. My car was legally parked as it backed into the other vehicle.
13. I saw a slow-moving, sad-faced old gentleman as he bounced off the roof of my car.
14. The telephone pole was approaching. As I was attempting to swerve out of its way, it struck the front of my car.
15. I pulled away from the side of the road, glanced at my mother-in-law, and headed over the embankment.
16. I told the police that I was not injured but, on removing my hat, found that I had a fractured skull.
17. The indirect cause of the accident was a little guy in a small car with a big mouth.
18. I had been driving 40 years when I fell asleep at the wheel and had an accident.
19. I had been shopping for plants all day and was on my way home. As I reached

the intersection, a hedge sprang up, obscuring my vision, and I did not see the other car.

20. I was thrown from my car as it left the road. I was later found in a ditch by some stray cows.

Heavenward ■ Use the whole group or, if your group is large, break into smaller teams of about 10 to 15 people. Give each team a balloon and explain that their task is to work together to touch the ceiling with their balloon. The only catch is that they can lift the balloon only by blowing it as a team. The first team to touch the ceiling with their balloon wins that round. Other rounds could include light items such as feathers, facial tissue, wax paper, etc.

This game illustrates how many people feel about their prayers—they only make it to the ceiling and then only after much effort.

Listening ■ Use three tape recorders (or a combination of TVs, radios, and tape recorders). Turn on all three—one should have music, another sound effects, and another someone speaking in a low voice. Have everyone listen for about three minutes. Then turn off the sounds and question them about what they heard. Make your questions quite specific.

Then have everyone get very quiet, shut their eyes, and just listen. After a minute or two, ask what they heard.

Another possibility is to give them a few mystery sounds to identify.

The point is that we can hear God speaking when we shut out the distractions and take time to listen.

P-R-A-I-S-E ■ Choose six kids and send them out of the room with the understanding that they will return, one at a time, and try to find a specific item in the room. The first person's item will begin with the letter *P* (e.g., penny, pencil, plate, package, person, etc.); the second person's would begin with *R* (e.g., radio, record, ring, etc.); and so on, spelling out the word *PRAISE*. As the person enters the room, the rest of the audience should clap louder as he or she comes closer to the specific item. The person to find his or her item the fastest wins.

Santa Claus ■ Introduce a special guest who got lost in the neighborhood a few weeks ago but would love to spend some time with them. Bring in Santa and seat him in front of the group. (Have fun with this—keep it light.) Explain that Santa will be glad to hear their Christmas requests for next Christmas as long as he's here. Ask them to think of one or two things that they most desire (give some examples, material and otherwise). Then have students come forward, one at a time, sit on Santa's lap, and tell him their requests. Secretly, have someone record all the requests. Later you may want to refer to this list, commenting on the nature of their requests.

The point is that often we treat God like a celestial "Santa Claus" who should grant all our desires. Our prayers sound a lot like our lists.

The Letter ■ Distribute cards and pencils to everyone. Each card should have a word written on it. Tell everyone to write one creative sentence, incorporating into it the word on the card. The sentence should describe a vacation. Possible words could include *beagle, bagel, bugle, scintillating, scuzzy, gregarious, lifeguard, green, threw up, froze, surfboard,* etc. Collect the cards, shuffle them, and then read them one at a time as a group letter. Begin by saying, "Dear (your name), My vacation has been great. . . ."

You can use this activity to introduce the topic of clear communication with God.

Trial Balloons ■ Give each person a balloon, a small piece of paper, and a pen. Have each one look around the room, choose one person, and write out a special wish for that person (they should not put their own names on the papers). Next, have them roll up their wish slips and place them inside the balloons. Then they should inflate and tie their balloons. At your signal, everyone should bat the balloons up to the ceiling and, as a group, try to keep them all airborne. After a minute or so, tell everyone to grab a balloon, pop it, and recover the slip inside. One at a time, have them stand and read the wishes.

This game should evoke good feelings and build group unity. It also illustrates how often our prayers don't seem to get beyond the ceiling—they just bounce back into our laps.

DISCUSSION STARTERS

Action ■ Give this assignment which you will discuss the following week: **This week, every day, I want you to have a time of prayer. During this time, the object will be to get to know God better. Use this format: five minutes of silence; five minutes of thanking and praising God for one of His attributes (take a different one each day); five minutes of meditating on the implications of that attribute to your life (and listening to God); five minutes of talking to God about those implications and applications. Keep a written record of what God is telling you about Himself and come next week ready to share.**

Note: If your group is not ready for an assignment this heavy, break it down into about five minutes a day, focusing on one part each day. Be sure to follow through and talk over their discoveries at the next meeting.

Assignment ■ Ask your group members to read a psalm or two each day for the next week, noting which ones are prayers and what those prayers involve.

Attributes ■ Before the meeting, ask six students to help you with this presentation. Give each of them one of the following attributes of God and have them come prepared with a biblical reference and a tangible example. Possible references and examples are given in parentheses.
■ Limitless (Psalm 8:3-4; a picture of the stars with statistics about the number of galaxies)
■ Personal (1 Samuel 13:14; John 15:12-17; a collage of pictures showing love)
■ Artistic (Job 38 and 39; Psalm 139:13-18; a collection of specimens from nature—a leaf, an insect, etc.)
■ Authoritative (Exodus 20:1-7; Hebrews 4:12; 2 Timothy 3:16; a few books from the pastor's library)
■ Mysterious (John 1:18; 1 Corinthians 2:9; pictures of clouds or stained-glass windows)
■ Loving (Romans 8:38-39; 1 John 4:7-8; a cross or picture of Jesus on the cross)
After each student has made his or her presentation, discuss as a whole group how they have experienced this attribute of God in their lives. Then have someone offer a prayer of thanks to God for that attribute.

Clichés ■ Read this series of clichés and after each one ask what is really meant by the phrase and how it limits God.

- He hasn't got a prayer! (Prayer is a last ditch effort to save someone; God may help you if you're desperate.)
- On a wing and a prayer (Prayer is like wishful thinking; God is like a good-luck charm.)
- The "Hail Mary" pass (An extreme combination of the two listed above.)
- The family that prays together, stays together. (The act itself is like glue; because it is a personal, close experience, God doesn't really have to be a part of it.)

Ask your students if they can think of any other appropriate clichés, and then continue the analysis.

Make it clear that each of these clichés contains some truth, but they are incomplete. If our understanding of God is limited to these, we really don't know Him at all. If our prayers are limited to these, we don't pray very well.

Definitions ■ As kids enter the room, give the early arrivers index cards and have each person write a definition of *praise.* Before the meeting, write out a dictionary definition on another card. Choose two or three of their best definitions and mix them with the one from the dictionary. Later in the meeting, as part of the discussion, see if they can guess which definition is the "official" one. Then discuss how we can truly praise God in worship, in prayer, and in our lives.

Group Prayer ■ Divide into groups and give each group a piece of paper and a pencil. Tell them to write a prayer for the whole group using only two or three sentences. Their prayers should be very specific. After a couple of minutes, have the prayers read. Then discuss how they felt about praying for the whole group using just a few sentences. Ask how this compares to our personal prayers which tend to be short and general.

Hello, Jesus ■ Ask: **If Jesus were here tonight, standing in front of you, and you could say one thing to Him, what would you say?** Discuss this for a short time. Then point out how this is similar to prayer—it is conversation with a person. Explain that Christ is here and we can talk to Him.

Praise Songs ■ Use the church hymnal or another songbook to lead the group in a series of praise songs. Songs and Creations, Inc. (P.O. Box 7, San Anselmo, CA 94960) is a great resource—their songbook has 82 selections listed under "praise." Then discuss why we call these "praise" songs and how they help us praise and worship God.

Praise Thoughts ■ Use the following outline as a framework for a discussion or for a wrap-up on praise.
1. Praise is not just in words to myself and others but in how I act.
2. Praising others can be difficult, but even a small amount of sincere praise will lead to greater reasons for praise.
3. Praise to God is commanded in Scripture, and it often involves singing. (See Psalm 150 and Revelation.)
4. Praise is a vital part of any healthy relationship, including our relationship with God.
5. Praise should be a natural response to what we know about God and His goodness.
6. Praise gets our eyes off ourselves and onto God.
7. Real praise is not flattery ("Hallowed be thy name").
8. Praise should be a habit—every day and in every situation.

Write a Prayer ■ Using groups of three or four kids, assign each group to write one of the parts of prayer (adoration and praise, confession, thanksgiving, supplication for others, supplication for self). After a few minutes, bring the whole group back together and read the prayer, one section at a time. If you can, copy it and distribute it to everyone.

DISCUSSIONS

Communication ■ To introduce this discussion, say: **Tonight we've been discussing prayer. This should be an easy topic to discuss because we all claim to be pray-ers. Some of us, however, feel like our prayers don't get past the ceiling.**

Others have experienced prayers similar to a visit with Santa Claus—we see God as someone who dishes out goodies for our enjoyment. Still others of us believe deeply in prayer, but we never seem to find time to spend quality time listening and talking with God.

Whatever your situation, here are a few thoughts on what real prayer should be.

The simplest definition of prayer is "talking with God." In other words, prayer is communication.

Now use the following outline as the framework for your discussion.

1. *Effective communication involves a clear relationship.* In any relationship, all barriers and blocks need to be removed before there can be effective communication. If you have lied to your parents recently, you'll have a difficult time talking to them; if you have just had a fight with your boyfriend or girlfriend, you probably won't be talking at all; and so on. The same is true with God. To have effective communication with Him, we need to clear the air, confess our sins and shortcomings, and remove the barriers to a good relationship.

2. *Effective communication takes time.* It is impossible to have a deep conversation with someone in bits and pieces, a minute or two a day. We know that won't work in our human relationships, but often we expect it to be effective with God. Real prayer involves "chatting" all day with Him and setting aside other times for longer talks.

3. *Effective communication involves honesty.* No one likes a phony, and most of us would rather not spend much time talking with someone who is playing a role, bragging, or rationalizing. Sometimes we try to "snow" God. That's kind of silly, actually, because He knows our very thoughts and motives. If we really want Him to work in our lives and to answer our prayers, we must honestly share our real thoughts and deepest feelings.

4. *Effective communication involves listening.* We have all been trapped in conversations where the other person does all the talking. It's frustrating. We feel as though they really don't care about what we have to say (when we do get that word in edgewise)—they are only waiting for their chance to speak again. A deep and meaningful prayer life will involve times of meditation on God's Word—just thinking about what we've read—and other times alone where we wait for God to speak to us. Sometimes we spend so much time talking and so little time listening because we're trying to talk God into doing our will instead of being willing to do His.

5. *Effective communication is two-way.* In other words, it's not just asking, but it's also giving and saying thank you. This two-way communication is a vital ingredient in prayer.

Our Father ■ Use the Lord's Prayer as the outline for your discussion. Take each phrase and discuss it: e.g., "What does it mean to call God 'our Father'?" "Where is heaven?" "Where is God—in heaven or here?" "What does 'hallowed' mean? How can we do that to God's name?" "How would our lives change if His will would be done in them?" Especially emphasize the "forgiving our debtors" phrase. Close by reciting the Lord's Prayer together.

Praise ■ Ask:
- **When do you find it difficult to praise someone? Why?**
- **When is it easy to praise someone? Why?**
- **When is it difficult to accept praise? Why?**
- **When is it easy to accept praise? Why?**
- **When is it difficult to praise God? Why? How can we praise God?**

Talking with God ■ Ask:
- **If prayer is "talking to God," how do our prayers help us get to know Him better?** (Usually they don't because we do all the talking, our mind wanders, and we don't listen. Our prayers could help us if we talked to Him about Him, thanked Him for His various attributes, and meditated on what we've learned in the Bible about God.)
- **Where would you look in the Bible for a good picture of what God is like? How about good examples of prayers?** (Jesus said that if we've seen Him, we've seen the Father. We can take a close look at Jesus, His life, and His prayers.)

BIBLE STUDIES

In Jesus' Name ■ Take time to explain briefly the basic parts of prayer—Adoration, Confession, Thanksgiving, Supplication (for others and self)—that spell out *ACTS*. Next, read John 14:13-14 and ask:
- **How does this verse relate to prayer?**
- **Does this really mean we can ask for anything?**
- **What does "in Jesus' name" mean?**
  Read John 16:23-26 and ask:
- **What does asking "in Jesus' name" mean here?**
- **What is complete joy?**

Prayer Groups ■ Use the following verses to get everyone into groups of 5 to 10. Type out the verses and then cut them up into various sections. Mix up all the pieces and distribute them. At your signal, the kids should get into their groups by matching up the verses. After you've read the verses aloud to make sure that every person is in the correct group, have each group discuss their specific verse to decide what the verse is teaching about prayer.
- Matthew 6:7 (vain repetition)
- Matthew 21:21-22 (pray and receive)
- 1 Thessalonians 5:16-17 (pray without ceasing)
- Colossians 4:2 (devote yourselves to prayer)
- James 5:14-16 (pray for the sick)

Psalms ■ Distribute copies of Psalm 150 and read it aloud together. Use other psalms as examples and ask what they teach us about the nature of praise.

The Bible on Prayer ■ Pass out these verses to various students. Have them read aloud, one at a time, and discuss each one.

■ Joshua 1:8 (We should meditate on God's Word.)
■ Psalm 46:10 (We must be quiet at times to really know God.)
■ Psalm 55:17 (We should pray regularly.)
■ Matthew 5:44 (We should pray for our enemies.)
■ Matthew 6:5-7 (We should pray secretly and honestly.)
■ Matthew 6:9-15 (Prayer implies relationship—"Father.")
■ Matthew 26:41 (Prayer will keep us from sin.)
■ Luke 18:1 (Prayer will give us courage.)
■ John 16:23-24 (Prayer involves asking.)
■ 1 Thessalonians 5:16-18 (We should pray at all times, giving thanks.)
■ James 5:13-14 (We should pray for those with deep needs.)
   Add others.

10
WORLD CONCERN AND SOCIAL ACTION

CROWD-BREAKERS

Double Matching ■ Prepare a matching quiz using the format below. List countries in the middle column and mix up "facts" and "problems" in their respective columns. Tie the problems to current events. For example, the fact for Lebanon could be "was called the 'Paris' of the Middle East," and the problem could be "terrible civil war." The fact for Northern Ireland could be, "known for potatoes," and the problem could be " 'Christian' vs. 'Christian.' " Students should put the number of the fact and the letter of the problem by the correct country.

Facts	Countries	Problems
1.		a.
2.		b.
3.		c.
4.		d.

First-World Scavenger Hunt ■ The goal of this game is to demonstrate how much we have and how much we take for granted.

This game can be played individually or in teams. Have everyone take out their wallets or purses. Then explain that you will call out a series of items. Each time they should search their (or their team's) belongings, find the item, and bring it to you. The first person to bring the item called wins that round. The winner is the person or team winning the most rounds. Here are some possible items to call.

■ a $20 bill
■ a ticket stub
■ a designer shirt
■ a picture of a house
■ evidence of a recent purchase of over $50

- a rubber band from someone's braces
- someone who has taken a trip by plane during the last month
- a piece of gold jewelry
- perfume
- a pizza coupon
- car keys
- a voter's registration card

You may want to comment about these evidences of our collective wealth.

Global Scavenger Hunt ■ Distribute bags to individuals or small teams of two or three and allow 20 or 30 minutes to find items representing as many countries as possible. These items may be found inside the building, outside, in a store, etc.; and they may include food (e.g., Turkish taffy), clothes (e.g., Mexican sombrero), pictures, (e.g., a postcard from England), appliances (e.g., Sony Walkman made in Japan), puns (e.g., "grease" = "Greece"), etc. After everyone has returned, display the items and award a prize to the winning team or individual.

Globe-trotter Relay ■ Divide into teams and place a large map of the world on the wall. When you call out a country, each team's representative should run to the map, find the country, and plant his or her team's flag (a colored pin or piece of tape). The person to find the country first wins that round for his or her team. Repeat for as many rounds as you wish, using different team representatives each time. Countries could include Chad, Bangladesh, United Arab Emirates, Liechtenstein, Belize, Zimbabwe, Singapore, as well as some of the larger and better-known ones.

In Their Shoes ■ Divide the group into boy-girl couples (or at least pair bigger kids with smaller ones). Then explain that this is a race to see which couple can exchange shoes without using hands, run to the far wall and back while holding hands, and then put their own shoes back on (again, without using hands) the quickest.

It's a Small World ■ Pass out the following matching quiz without the answers. (The correct answers are in parentheses.)

IT'S A SMALL WORLD

Match each word with the correct country or nationality.

_____ Russian (h)	a.	checkers
_____ Siberian (i)	b.	spring
_____ Hong Kong (e)	c.	measles
_____ Chinese (a)	d.	knight
_____ Pole (k)	e.	flu
_____ Bermuda (g)	f.	pastries
_____ English (n)	g.	shorts
_____ French (v)	h.	roulette
_____ Turkish (p)	i.	huskie
_____ Mexican (x)	j.	twins
_____ Spanish (s)	k.	vault
_____ Jamaica (m)	l.	bacon
_____ Columbian (u)	m.	Joe
_____ Tazmanian (r)	n.	leather

_____ Brazil (z)	o.	tape
_____ Arabian (d)	p.	bath
_____ Norwegian (aa)	q.	tanker
_____ Brussels (y)	r.	devil
_____ Canadian (l)	s.	inquisition
_____ Swiss (w)	t.	hound
_____ Irish (b)	u.	coffee
_____ Scotch (o)	v.	toast
_____ German (c)	w.	cheese
_____ Afghan (t)	x.	hat dance
_____ Danish (f)	y.	sprouts
_____ Liberian (q)	z.	nut
_____ Siamese (j)	aa.	wood

My Cup Runneth Over ■ Divide into teams. Give each team a glass filled with colored liquid (to be placed at one end of the room), a smaller empty glass (to be placed at the other end of the room), and an eyedropper. Team members, one at a time, will fill the eyedropper at one end of the room, empty it in their glass at the other end and pass the eyedropper to the next teammate in line. The first team to overflow their glass wins. Note: Use a different color of water for each team, and make sure your liquids are non-staining.

Not-so-fast Food ■ Choose a few competitors (depending on how much pie you can afford) and explain that they will be involved in an eating contest. After everyone has been seated at the table in front of a piece of pie covered with ice cream, distribute sets of chop sticks which they must use to eat the food. The first person to eat all of the pie and ice cream wins.

Sense-tense ■ Divide into six teams and assign each team a _number_ and a _word_. Explain that when you hold up their group's number, they are to stand as a group and shout out their word. (Their number may be used more than once.) Here are the numbers and words: 1—want; 2—and; 3—I; 4—all; 5—need; 6—have. Practice once by going in order; the sentence will make no sense. Read the following sentences by the numbers, one at a time, pausing after each one to see if they heard what the whole group said. The sentences are:
■ 3, 1, 4, 3, 6, 2, 5—I want all I have and need.
■ 3, 1, 1, 1, 4—I want, want, want all!
■ 2, 5, 3, 6, 4, 3, 1—And need I have all I want?
■ 6, 3, 5, . . .3, 1, 4—Have I need? I want all!
■ 3, 5, 4, 3, 1, 2, 6—I need all I want and have.
■ 4, 3, 1, 2, 5, 3, 6—All I want and need I have.
If they get the hang of it early, you can speed up with each succeeding sentence. After the last one, review the sentences and ask if they ever feel this way. Point out that we have so much, but often we cling to it and want more.

Spin the Globe ■ Bring a globe that can be spun on its axis. Choose a number of volunteers who will close their eyes (or be blindfolded), spin the globe, and stop the spin by placing a finger on the globe. Assign the player a task related to place pointed to. At first, make this light and fun, giving a humorous task for each ocean and continent (e.g., for landing in the Caribbean, sing a reggae song or do the limbo; for landing in Egypt, walk like an Egyptian). Later (or the second round), have players tell about the countries in which their fingers land—what needs have they heard of there or near there? If they land in an ocean, they could talk about the boat people, the Haitian refugees, etc. (Come prepared with a list of countries and needs.) The point is that the world is filled with needy people—how aware are we and what are we doing about it?

DISCUSSION STARTERS

Actions ■ Conclude a meeting by encouraging students to choose two actions—a personal commitment (to reach out to the "nerd-like" kid at school, to help a handicapped student, to become a pen pal to a missionary kid overseas, to tutor a slower student, to help at home, etc.) and a group commitment (to sponsor an orphan overseas, to send "care packages" to missionary families, to form a youth group coalition to meet specific community needs through special projects, to "adopt" grandparents in nursing homes, to work with the student council to sponsor quality assembly programs, etc.).

Amnesty International ■ Read aloud a few of their reports on repression, torture, and other atrocities as a catalyst for discussion and prayer.

Atmosphere ■ On the wall, hang provocative pictures of human needs (e.g., a hungry child, a person in prison, someone experiencing grief, a person walking all alone). At some point in the meeting, point to each one and discuss what these people are feeling, how Christians should respond to them, whether we know people like these, what we can do to help them, etc.

Challenge ■ Use this outline as a wrap-up or discussion catalyst.
1. The real world is filled with hungry and oppressed people. It is bigger than our families, community, and country.
2. There are hurting people right near us.
3. The Christian faith is not "fantasy" or only "pie in the sky," but must be applied now in this *real* world.
4. This application means showing God's love, joy, and peace in our lives in deeper ways than religious clichés and froth, and reaching out to others with love.

Getting Involved ■ Go through newspapers or current news magazines and clip out stories of hijackings, bombings, unjust imprisonments, kidnappings, and other human rights violations. Pass out the stories and have students summarize them aloud for the whole group. Then ask them what they can do to make a difference in the world—right now. Here are some possibilities:
■ Become informed.
■ Pray for the persecuted and the persecutors.
■ Write government leaders in the countries involved.
■ Write congressional representatives, asking them to intervene, put pressure on, and help.
■ Send money, clothing, etc., where it will be useful.

Giving Collage ■ Divide into three groups and give each group a stack of magazines, scissors, a role of tape, and a piece of poster board. Their assignment is to create collages (one per group) out of pictures found in the magazines according to their assigned theme.
■ Group 1—self-centeredness

- Group 2—world needs
- Group 3—helping hurting people

After everyone has finished, have the groups display and explain their works of art. Then ask:

- **How difficult was it to find pictures to fit your theme?**
- **Which group had the easiest time? Why?**
- **What if a magazine were published of your school; which theme would be the most prominent? Why?**
- **What if a magazine were published of you; what would it look like? Why?**

Good News ■ Play the Anne Murray song "A Little Good News" (from the album of the same name, Capitol Records, Inc.) and ask:

- **What kind of bad news does Anne Murray mention in the song?**
- **This song was written a few years ago—were any of those things in the news today? Which ones?**
- **What difference can just one person make in the world today?**
- **What difference could a *group* of Christians make in the world today?**
- **What difference could *our* group of Christians make in the world today?**

Inscription ■ This inscription was found in Lubeck Cathedral. Read it and then discuss it or have someone read it to end the meeting.

You call me Master—and obey me not.
You call me Light—and see me not.
You call me Way—and walk me not.
You call me Life—and desire me not.
You call me Wise—and follow me not.
You call me Rich—and ask me not.
You call me Fair—and love me not.
You call me Eternal—and seek me not.
You call me Gracious—and trust me not.
You call me Noble—and serve me not.
You call me Mighty—and honor me not.
You call me Just—and fear me not.
If I condemn you—blame me not.

Interview ■ Invite some international students and ask them to share their experiences living in the United States. Ask:

- **What did you expect to find when you came to the U.S.?**
- **How did your experience differ from these expectations?**

A visiting foreign missionary would be a great interview subject; change the questions to apply to his or her mission country.

Missionaries ■ Bring the names of missionary kids (especially junior and senior highers) and stationery and have your young people write letters to them.

Missionary Map ■ If you have a youth room, post a large world map with various missionaries and other overseas contacts marked on it with pins, pictures, etc. From time to time, highlight one of these missionaries and pray for him or her.

Missions Conference ■ Design a missions conference for your group. Bring in special speakers, show informative films, have displays, and write to missionary kids.

Music ■ Play one or more contemporary songs dealing with global problems and concerns and discuss the lyrics and the possible motives for writing and performing them. Song options include secular renditions ("Do They Know It's Christmas?" by Band Aid; "We Are the World" by USA for Africa; and "Tears Are Not Enough" by Northern Lights) and Christian songs (including "Do Something Now" by CAUSE; Gary Rand's album "Songs for the Jubilee"; Ken Medema's album "Kingdom in the Streets"; Petra's "Hollow Eyes"; and many others).

News Flash ■ Distribute newspapers from a variety of cities and countries if possible (most of them should be written in English) and have everyone look for stories about problems in foreign countries. These they should cut out and form into a group collage. Spend a few minutes discussing how Christians should respond in each situation and how they themselves would respond if they were living there. Then have them share experiences which they've had in the countries named and tell about any people they know there.

Potluck ■ Sponsor an international potluck dinner where individual young people (or groups of kids) make and bring the dishes to eat.

Prayer ■ Before a meeting, prepare on index cards short summaries of the special needs of individual missionaries that your church is supporting. Include as much information as possible (one missionary per card). Then break into small groups, give each group a card, and spend a time in prayer for your missionaries.

Prayer List ■ Keep a group prayer list of "large" concerns (not specific, individual requests). Include on this list world missions and the problem areas of the world. Spend time praying for these various needs in your meetings.

Quiz ■ Hand out the following "anti" quiz, without the answers (correct answers are in parentheses).

FAMOUS "ANTI'S"

1. medicine	anti_____	(antibiotic)
2. look forward to	anti_____	(anticipate)
3. counteracts poison	anti_____	(antidote)
4. radiator filler	anti_____	(antifreeze)
5. protein	anti_____	(antigen)
6. daughter of Oedipus	Anti_____	(Antigone)
7. helpful with a cold	anti_____	(antihistamine)
8. a definite dislike	anti_____	(antipathy)
9. exact opposite	anti_____	(antipode or antithesis)
10. unsociable	anti_____	(antisocial)
11. preventing infection	anti_____	(antiseptic)
12. prejudiced against Jews	anti_____	(anti-Semitic)
13. opposed to monopolies	anti_____	(antitrust)
14. ancient, old	anti_____	(antique or antiquated)
15. British island in the West Indies	Anti_____	(Antigua)

After giving the correct answers and determining the winner, explain that, unfortunately, many Christians are known by their "anti's." Then have the students list all the things that Christians are against. As each one is mentioned, discuss briefly whether or not it is good to be for or against that particular thing. (The list could include drinking, abortion, evolution, secular humanism, dancing, pornography, crime, cheating, premarital sex, etc.)

Ask: **Do you think the negative image of Christianity is justified? Why or why not?**

Next ask what the New Testament says Christians should be for. Ask for specific evidence for each one, and list these qualities or causes on the chalkboard or poster board. (The list could include love, truth, forgiveness, human rights, honesty, justice, family, marriage, health, healing, hope, morality, faith, and personal development and growth.)

Then say: **It's overwhelming, isn't it, what Christians are for and what they should be for! Unfortunately, however, the world has the opposite idea. Maybe they just haven't seen the evidence. What evidence can you see in our society for positive Christian action?** (Hospitals, schools, churches, missions, etc.) **In history?** (Abolitionist movement, Sunday school, education for orphans, higher education, etc.) **Across the world?** (Missionaries, Christian relief agencies, activists for human rights, etc.) **In this room?**

Refreshments ■ For refreshments, serve a variety of foreign foods (e.g., baklava or just a spoon of rice, etc.)

Resources ■ *The Mustard Seed Conspiracy* by Tom Sine (Word, 1981) has many helpful suggestions for group and individual involvement with problems of the poor and oppressed. Evangelicals for Social Action (ESA) and Prison Fellowship are organizations which can be helpful and which offer chances to serve. Youth for Christ has Project Serve, summer missions projects. Intercristo is an organization which matches Christians with service opportunities. World Vision International, Compassion, Care, World Relief, U.S. Center for World Missions, and other organizations will provide many helpful materials from countries and mission fields worldwide.

Servant Refreshments ■ At the end of the meeting, announce that you will be having "servant refreshments." That is, the kids may eat as much of the food as they wish, but they cannot serve themselves. They can only feed (and be fed by) someone else.

Sheep and Goats ■ Take the specific examples mentioned in Matthew 25 (hungry, thirsty, stranger, naked, sick, in prison) and arrange special field trips to observe these needs firsthand (e.g., take a tour of the local prison or jail, drive through skid row). After each trip, ask what the kids, as a group and as individuals, can do to help those people. Possible answers would include: write letters to prisoners, give money to those who are helping the poor and those on skid row, send food, collect clothes, pray. Make a group prayer list which reflects these special needs.

Starving and Sleeping ■ Play the song, "Starving Sinner, Sleeping Saint" from "Home Where I Belong" by B.J. Thomas. Wait a few seconds for the message to sink in and ask:
■ **What is a "starving sinner"? Do you know any?**
■ **How does this song picture some churches?**
■ **When are you a "sleeping saint"?**

Stewardship ■ Spend a meeting discussing stewardship of our lives and money. Help your kids design personal budgets giving special attention to the practice of tithing. Establish a group fund to give money to a special project at church or in the community.

Tangible Help ■ Focus on one specific need and have a work day to raise money for that project.

Up Close and Personal ■ Before the meeting, collect a number of pictures of young people from magazines and newspapers. Look for those which capture a bit of the individual's personality (not models). Mount them on separate pieces of cardboard. Then, one at a time, hold up the pictures for the whole group to see and ask them to imagine what the person is like. Use these questions to prod their thinking.

■ **What do this person's parents do for occupations?**
■ **What are this person's hobbies?**
■ **What career do you think this person will have?**
■ **What was this person's last meal?**
■ **Describe this person's family life.**

Here are some ideas for pictures. Use a variety and mix up the order in terms of affluence.

■ a well-dressed American boy
■ a Russian worker
■ a young Central American or South American soldier
■ an African farmer
■ a Japanese tourist
■ a black American in the city
■ a white American in a school
■ a Chinese child on a farm
■ a Lebanese in the Beirut rubble
■ an Ethiopian with the look of starvation

What I Have ■ Explain that you are going to have a type of scavenger hunt. Whoever has something that matches the description you call out should stand and display or describe the item (the item must be in the room).

Preface each question with: **What do you have . . .**

■ **that you received from your brother or sister?**
■ **that you received from an aunt or uncle?**
■ **that you received from a grandparent?**
■ **that you received from your boyfriend or girlfriend?**
■ **that you received from another friend?**
■ **that you received from a teacher?**
■ **that you received from your parent(s)?**
■ **that you received from God?**

At first, the only responses will be material (clothes, money, pictures, etc.). Other possibilities could include love, friendship, education, etc. Things received from parents and God could include hereditary characteristics such as looks, hair color, height, and others, and will get into less tangible areas such as security, personality, eternal life, forgiveness, happiness, and others.

Choose a winner, or go right into a discussion of what we have. The point is that all that we are and have are gifts from God, directly or through others—what are we giving to others?

DISCUSSIONS

Giving Back ■ Ask the group for ways that we can begin to "give back" some of what God has given to us. Record their answers on a chalkboard, poster board, or flip chart. Begin with major areas such as "home," "time," "money," and "expertise," and list specific ideas under each one. For example, ways to give back time to God could include having a "quiet time," spending time with grandparents, visiting rest homes, doing volunteer work, choosing a career of service, and so on.

Have-nots ■ Ask:
- What kind of image do you get of China from the news reports in papers and magazines and on television? Of Russia? Ethiopia? Haiti? Brazil? Mexico?
- How accurately do you think the media portray life in those countries? Why?
- How do you think life in America is portrayed by the press in those countries? How accurate is that portrayal? Why?
- How should America be portrayed to other countries? What is the truth about our wealth and abundance?
- If you lived in a very poor country, how would you feel about the United States if you knew of America's wealth and abundance?
- What can Americans do to help poor people in other countries?

Love List ■ Use this assignment to get material for a future meeting. Have everyone list the acts of unselfish love they observe around them during the next week. They should list at least one each day and try to list different acts. Discuss their findings at your next meeting.

Over There ■ Ask:
- Who do you know personally who has been to a foreign country? What did that person learn from the experience?
- Who do you know who is from another country? What is his or her religious background?
- What can you do to bring the Gospel to people in other lands?

Quick Draw ■ Give everyone a sheet of paper and a pen or pencil. Tell them to write their names on the top and to leave the rest of their sheets blank. Collect all the papers and then redistribute them, making sure that no one gets his or her own. After everyone has someone else's sheet, tell them to take a few minutes to think about that person and then to write on the paper what they think he or she has to offer to the world (positively)—the unique contribution that the person has to make. After a few minutes, collect the papers and return them to their owners. You may want to discuss the experience.

Showing Love ■ Pass out papers and pens or pencils to everyone. Have them write three ways that they could show unselfish love to each of the following persons during the next week:
- teacher
- friend
- enemy
- parent
- neighbor

- employer
- sibling

Wrap-up ■ Emphasize the following points in a wrap-up or in your discussion.
1. Our lives model our true faith—what we really believe.
2. Our lives are so full, but often we still hoard what we have, even our overflow.
3. Our selfish hoarding attitude speaks loud and clear.
4. The world is filled with people who need Christ and who need us.
5. In reality, all that we are and have are gifts that we are to use wisely.
6. Instead of being "sleeping saints," (see the discussion starter **Starving and Sleeping**) we should wake up and give to others, responding in love and in obedience to God's Word.

Then propose possible group projects such as going on a summer mission trip like Project Serve (Youth for Christ), having a planned famine (World Vision), adopting an orphan (Compassion), raising money for the needy of your community, visiting regularly the nursing home, and others.

Have the group choose one, and distribute cards so that they can sign up and indicate their commitment to the project.

BIBLE STUDIES

Adopt a Neighbor ■ Study the parable of The Good Samaritan (Luke 10:25-37) and discuss the question of who our neighbors are. Ask the pastor for the names of people in the church or community who have needs that your group could meet (e.g., mow the lawn, rake the leaves, shovel the snow, prepare and take meals, clean the house, take to church, visit in nursing homes or hospitals).

Faith Demonstration ■ Type up James 2:14-19 and give copies to six young people (each sheet should have one verse highlighted). Ask them to read their verses, in order, with feeling. After they read, ask:
- **What does James mean in these verses? What is his message?**
- **How do people know that you and I have faith in Christ?**
- **What can we do to demonstrate our faith?**

Goats and Sheep ■ Have a guy and a girl read Matthew 25:31-46, with the girl reading the first half (verses 31-40) and the guy reading the second half (verses 41-46). Distribute cards and pencils and have everyone answer these questions individually:
1. What made the difference between the sheep and the goats?
2. Based on your life-performance so far, what would you be—a sheep or a goat?
3. List one situation where you could act like a sheep.

Collect the cards and read their answers to question 2 aloud without indicating the identity of the person. Then read a few answers for question 3. Discuss the experience: how they would feel in that kind of situation and what action they should take.

Love ■ Read John 13:34-35 aloud. Then ask:
- **What is the main point of these verses? Why would this be such a dramatic evidence of our belonging to Christ?**
- **How do these verses relate to others who aren't Christians? How can we show Christ's love to others?**

Salt and Light ■ Have a student read Matthew 5:13-16 aloud. Then ask the group to give the attributes and qualities of both salt and light. List their answers on the board. After compiling the list, ask how each of these qualities is relevant to the Christian life. In other words, how can Christians really be "salt" and "light" in the world?

Here are some possible answers:

■ Salt is used as seasoning—Christians can bring flavor to the world through their love, joy, etc.

■ Salt is used as a preservative (kept meat from spoiling in the first century)—Christians should be a preserving force for good, holding back the rot of sin.

■ Salt is used to melt ice—Christians can melt the cold barriers which divide people from each other and from God through love, friendship, and compassion.

■ Salt is used as a healing agent—Christians are called to help heal the physical and spiritual hurts in their communities and the world.

■ Light is used to show the way—Christians should show the way to eternal life.

■ Light is used to spotlight—Christians should focus attention on Christ.

■ Light is used to signal and warn—Christians should warn of the consequences of sin.

Discuss various "bushels" and challenge the students to let their lights shine. Then turn off the lights, light a single candle in the center of the group, and sing together prayerfully "Pass it On" or "This Little Light of Mine."

The Bible Says . . . ■ Type the following verses on separate index cards and number them. Distribute the cards and have individuals read the verses aloud, one at a time, in numerical order. Make no comments until all the passages have been read.

1. Amos 2:6-7a
2. Deuteronomy 15:10-11
3. Psalm 109:30-31
4. Psalm 146:5-7
5. Revelation 3:17-18
6. Psalm 73:12
7. James 5:1-6
8. Luke 4:18-19
9. Luke 14:12-14
10. Luke 18:22
11. Matthew 25:42-46
12. 2 Corinthians 8:9
13. Philippians 2:4-8

Then ask:

■ **How do you feel after hearing all of these verses?**

■ **What is God telling us to do?**

■ **How do you think you can make a contribution toward solving these problems?**

The Least of These ■ Read Matthew 25:31-46 aloud. Then ask:

■ **Does this passage apply to us today? Why or why not?**

■ **How does this passage relate to the worldwide needs which we have heard about? How can we respond to them. Who is responsible for solving the problems with human rights and human needs?**

■ **Here at home, who is hungry? Sick? In prison? How can we respond to these people?**

What Christians Are For ■ Break into small groups and give each group one of the following passages. Have them discuss the positive implication of each passage. In other words, what are the verses saying Christians should do?

1. 1 Corinthians 13:1 and 1 John 3:16-18 (love)
2. Matthew 5:13-16 (be "salt" and "light")
3. Philippians 2:4-11 (be humble)
4. James 2:14-19 (give to those in need)
5. Matthew 25:34-40 (respond to poverty, injustice, etc.)
6. Luke 6:37-38 (forgive)

Have the groups report their findings, and then discuss how they can apply these in specific ways in their lives.

11
COMPETITION

CROWD-BREAKERS

Children's Games ■ Because you are emphasizing competition, the crowd will be enthusiastically involved in whatever games you choose. Therefore, simple children's games (schoolyard games or purchased games or puzzles) can be very effective. Do them as relays or as head-to-head competition between team representatives.

De Agony of De-Feet ■ In this relay team members must pass a variety of items down the line, person to person, using prescribed parts of the body. Give each team the same items to pass and let them decide how they will pass each item. The team finishing first wins. Here are the rounds.
■ "de-feet" (items may be passed only between each person's feet)
■ "de-arms" (items may be passed only between each person's arms—no hands allowed)
■ "de-elbows"
■ "de-chins and necks"
■ "de-little fingers"
■ "de-hips"
■ "de-knees"
  Items to pass could include bananas, marshmallows, marbles, water balloons, soccer balls, "Play Doh," etc.

Gatorade Chug ■ As the name implies, this is a contest to see who can drink a glass of Gatorade the quickest. Because this is not the most tasty drink, don't let contestants know what they will be drinking until the game begins. Use team representatives—the first person finished wins. If you have time, you may want to do two rounds—one for the guys and one for the girls.

Hungry Hippos ■ This is a child's game which may be purchased in any toy store. It features four plastic hippos which are competing to devour as many marbles as possible. Place the game on a card table in the center of the room. Using team representatives, compete in a series of "hippo matches." The individual to capture the most marbles wins that match for his or her team. Give the winning team 4 points, second place 3 points, third place 2, and fourth place 1. Hold additional matches with new team reps. The team to win the most points after 5 or 6 rounds wins the game.

Hurdles ■ Before the meeting, build little "hurdles" out of popsicle sticks or small pieces of wood and paint them with marking pens to make them look official. (Make enough hurdles to replace any that get broken during the game.) Have each team choose a representative to compete (a big guy would be best). Using large rubber bands or rope, tie each competitor's knees together. Then, at your signal, he or she is to run the course, jumping over the hurdles which you have placed on the floor. Time each contestant individually, adding 5 seconds for each hurdle knocked down and 20 seconds for each one broken. The fastest person wins.

Spelling Bee ■ Have each team send a representative to the front to compete in an old-fashioned "spelling bee." Begin by asking contestants to spell easy, three-letter words, and gradually move to more difficult ones. Award points for first, second, and third places.

Superlative ■ Divide into teams for this variation of a scavenger hunt. Each team will choose someone from their team who meets your announced description. When all the teams' representatives have assembled at the front, you will determine a winner for that round and proceed with the next round. Here are some descriptions to use for the different rounds:
■ the tallest member of your team (award points to the team who sends to you the tallest person of all the team representatives)
■ the person with the longest hair
■ the person with the smallest feet
■ the person with the most money in his or her wallet or purse
■ the person with the straightest teeth
■ the person with the darkest hair
■ the strongest (hold a quick arm-wrestling or timed push-ups competition to determine the winner)
   This game demonstrates how we often compete in our society. You may want to refer to this in your discussion or wrap-up.

Teams and Cheers ■ As kids enter the room, play the "Super Bowl Shuffle," "Theme from Chariots of Fire," "Theme from Rocky," "Eye of the Tiger," "Victory" by Kool and the Gang, or another "competitive" song in the background to set the mood. Divide into teams by classes, alphabet, birthdays, or at random and tell each team to make up a cheer for their team. After a few minutes have them cheer, then move into your other games.

The Greatest ■ Explain that this game is an individual as well as a team contest, and offer a prize to the individual who gets all the answers correct (and a team prize for the group with the highest total of correct answers). Then hand out the following quiz. They should match the correct sport or talent with the prize or competition (the correct answers are in parentheses).

Sport or Talent	Prize or Competition
_____ golf (k)	a. Belmont Stakes
_____ writing (l)	b. Super Bowl
_____ drag racing (j)	c. America's Cup
_____ movies/acting (i)	d. Stanley Cup
_____ football (b)	e. Tony
_____ music (o)	f. Davis Cup
_____ horse racing (a)	g. Indy 500
_____ plays/acting (e)	h. World Cup
_____ professional basketball (m)	i. Oscar
_____ baseball (r)	j. Grand Nationals
_____ hockey (d)	k. Ryder Cup
_____ television/acting (q)	l. Pulitzer Prize
_____ sailing (c)	m. N.B.A. Championship
_____ college basketball (p)	n. W.B.A. Championship
_____ tennis (f)	o. Grammy
_____ soccer (h)	p. Final Four
_____ auto racing (g)	q. Emmy
_____ boxing (n)	r. World Series

Tiny Bubbles ■ Before the meeting, prepare as a target a board or piece of cardboard with a 4-inch hole in the center of it. Also, purchase bubble-blowing liquid and makers. The idea of this game is for one team member to make bubbles while the other team members blow them toward the target. Each bubble to pass through the hole is worth a point. The team to get the most points in two minutes wins. This can also be done as a relay.

DISCUSSION STARTERS

Basic Competition ■ Use these thoughts to stimulate discussion or to wrap up a meeting.

Competion is basic to America. It is integral to our economy (the free-enterprise system), and our history is filled with striving to be the best and the greatest. Competition can be healthy if we compete against ourselves or a standard of quality—then we should try to do and be the very best we can. But competition can be unhealthy and even destructive when we compete with others and become obsessed with getting ahead of "them." So often our egos are tied to our achievements—at every football or basketball game, partisans on the winning side raise their index fingers high and shout, "We're number one!" We can feel as though we are failures if we are not the fastest, most attractive, smartest, or whatever.

Competition—Pros and Cons ■ Use the following outline for a discussion guide or a wrap-up. Add local and personal illustrations where appropriate.
1. _Competition is a way of life in America_—we hold everything from Miss America pageants to "Super Bowls" to determine who is the greatest in some area. We seem obsessed with being "number 1." We even talk about being "the greatest nation on earth" as though it were a contest.
2. _Competition can be good if it motivates us to be better, to excel—if we_

compete against a standard or against ourselves.

3. *Competition can be bad and destructive if we compete only against others, having to be better than they are.* This is bad because it gives us a wrong idea of our worth (we feel worthless when we lose and prideful when we win). It is destructive when we hurt, cheat, or push others down to push ourselves up or to make ourselves look good.

4. *Competition reflects our values.* Our world puts a high priority on money, beauty, power, strength, and youth; therefore, the "winners" excel in these areas. Jesus' values, however, are quite different. Look at Matthew 5:3-12 for His list. It includes "poor in spirit," "mourners," "meek," "hungry for righteousness," "merciful," "pure in heart," "peacemakers," "persecuted for righteousness," and others. People with these qualities come in dead last in our society; but in God's eyes, they are first.

5. *Be careful with competition.* Remember, everything in this world lasts for only a moment, but God's kingdom lasts forever. Keep your focus on doing what He wants. As Duane Thomas, running back for the Super Bowl Champion Dallas Cowboys, said a few years ago, "If this game is the ultimate, why do we play it every year?"

6. *Find your value in God, not in how good you look or how well you perform.* You are very special to Him—He created you, and He loves you.

The Prize ■ After a number of games, announce that you are going to proclaim the winning team. Read off the point totals and then pronounce the team with the least points the winner. Calm everyone down and read Mark 9:33-37 aloud. Then ask:

■ **According to this verse, wouldn't it be right to give the prize to the team with the least number of points? Why or why not?**

■ **What did Jesus mean when He said that whoever wants to be first must be last?**

■ **How is this different from what our society says?**

DISCUSSIONS

Coaches ■ Spend a few minutes discussing various types of coaches (well-known ones in the college and professional ranks and coaches they've had in junior and senior high school).

Next, discuss which coach brought out the best in them as team members and as people. Finally, ask what they think about God as a coach:

■ **What kind of coach would He be?**

■ **Is this a good illustration of what God is like?**

■ **How would He motivate us to do our best?**

Good or Bad? ■ Ask:

■ **Is competition good or bad and why?**

■ **When have you been helped by competition?**

■ **When have you been hurt?**

■ **Why do you think it is so important for some people to win? (Some of you got pretty involved in our silly games tonight!)**

■ **Besides games and sports, how else do we compete?** (Looks, grades, status, etc.)

■ **What does the Bible say about competition?**

BIBLE STUDIES

Coach ■ Look up the following passages together. After each one, ask how this characteristic of God fits into the concept of Him as a coach. (Note: sometimes God is more of a cheerleader than a coach to us.)
1. 1 John 2:1-2
2. 1 Corinthians 1:27
3. Romans 8:31-33
4. Matthew 5:38-39
5. Mark 10:44-45
6. 1 John 4:8
7. Romans 8:1

Last and First ■ Divide into groups and give each group one of the passages listed below. Have them discuss what Jesus meant and how it relates to competition.
1. Matthew 19:26-30
2. Matthew 22:37-40
3. Matthew 25:1-13
4. Matthew 25:31-40
5. Mark 9:33-35
6. Mark 10:29-31
7. Mark 10:35-45

NOTE:
Following are four designs for whole meetings centered on the competition theme. Each one includes games, discussion questions, and a wrap-up outline.

NONCOMPETITIVE GAMES

The New Games Book (Doubleday/Dolphin) is a good resource for games which stress having fun where everyone wins. There are many types of activities included for outdoors, indoors, large groups, small groups, etc. Instead of (or in addition to) these games, the meeting could feature regular competitive games altered so that everyone wins, or games that favor smaller, less athletic individuals.

Outdoor games could include touch rugby, "blind volleyball" (played with regular volleyball rules except that no spiking is allowed, and with blankets draped over the net so that players can't see the ball until it comes on their side), "maximum volleyball" (the ball must be hit by at least 5 different members of the team before it can be returned), or kick ball.

Indoor possibilities could include reverse charades (a team representative must guess which word or phrase his or her team is acting out), sit-down tug-of-war, and others.

Discussion Questions
■ **What was unusual about the games we played?**
■ **How do you feel about not having a clear-cut winner and loser?**
■ **What does this say about the relationship between fun and competition?**
■ **Paul uses the analogy of sports (Philippians 3:12-26). How does this relate to competition?**

Wrap-up

1. Paul is saying that the overwhelming motivation for his life is to be the kind of person God wants him to be, no matter what others may think or do.

2. Too often we use others to help us feel good about ourselves. That is, their acceptance of us in the clique will enhance the way we feel. Or perhaps we compare ourselves to "losers" and look pretty good. Competition often reveals these feelings. It's part of our society and of our lives. We seem to be continually competing with others and with ourselves, and we never really accomplish what God wants for us.

3. God's plan is for us to keep our eyes on Christ. He is the only one whose approval really counts (He accepts us and loves us as we are), and He will never let us down. If we keep our eyes on Him and follow His direction, increasingly we will become the kind of people that God wants us to be.

4. This kind of relationship with God will free us to relax with and to accept others. We won't see them as winners or losers or as competitors, but as fellow human beings whom God loves and for whom Christ died.

COMPETITION IN EVERY AREA

Design a meeting to involve competition in the four areas of life: physical, mental, social, and spiritual. Here are some possibilities.

PHYSICAL COMPETITION

Eating Contests ■ Divide into teams and choose a representative from each team to eat the most pie within 30 seconds, no hands allowed, or to eat a peach and leave the cleanest pit, without hands. Choose a couple from each team, blindfold them, and at the signal have them feed each other corn on the cob or some other comparably messy food. Challenge someone to eat a raw egg or to swallow a live goldfish.

Strength Contests ■ See who can pick up a chair by using only one hand and gripping the chair near the base of one leg. Design a unique strength test like pulling a heavy rubber band until it breaks, or wrap a person in thread and time how long it takes to break out.

MENTAL COMPETITION

College Bowl ■ Choose representatives from each team to compete in a "college bowl" contest. Then ask tricky questions like "How many three-cent stamps in a dozen?" (These can be found in the booklet *How Many Three Cent Stamps in a Dozen* by Herman Hoover: Price/Stern/Sloan, 1979.)

Puzzle ■ Compose a word puzzle which includes the names of students in your group. The names may be written horizontally, vertically, diagonally, backward, or forward. See who can find the most names.

Trivia ■ Design a trivia quiz from the high school (e.g., Who was last year's homecoming queen? Who was this year's right guard on the football team? What's the name of the assistant principal? What's the color of the cafeteria chairs? Who is the editor of the school newspaper? etc.).

SOCIAL COMPETITION

Best Friends ■ Choose sets of best friends and see how much they really know about each other. Ask questions about birthplace, middle names, favorite foods, etc.

Friends Bingo ■ Prepare a bingo-type card for everyone with all the spaces blank. Each person must get signatures for every space from kids in the room. Then call out names just as you would the letters and numbers in bingo.

The Most ■ See who knows the names of the most people in the group.

SPIRITUAL COMPETITION

Bible Books ■ Choose representatives from teams and have them put a list of Bible books (written on cards) in the proper order. Throw in a few fictitious ones like "Hezekiah" and "Hesitations" to confuse them.

Characters ■ Give each team a little-known Bible character and have them tell everything they know about him or her. Use people like Gomer, Eutychus, Zipporah, Cleopas, etc.

Definitions ■ Give each team a theological word and have them write a definition for it. Use words like *propitiation, supralapsarianism,* and *lasciviousness.*

Discussion Questions
■ **Did you notice anything unusual about our games tonight?** (You competed physically, mentally, socially, and spiritually.)
■ **In real life, how do we compete in these areas?**
■ **Why do you think we have a need to compete?** (To feel good about ourselves; to please our parents or peers; etc.)
■ **How should God's feeling about you as a person affect your need to compete?**

Wrap-up
1. Competition is an integral part of our society. The free-enterprise system thrives on it, democracy uses it, and we are all affected by it.
2. The problem is that competition emphasizes a world view which is opposite to the one taught by Christ. The world says power and prestige are important; the Bible teaches humility (Philippians 2:3-11). The world says we should accumulate wealth and honors; Jesus tells us to give up everything and follow Him (Luke 18:18-30). The world teaches us to look out for our own interests, making sure that no one puts us down; Jesus says we are to love others as much as we love ourselves (Matthew 22:39). The world states that we should strive for importance and popularity; Jesus tells us to serve others (John 13:12-20). The world exalts winners; Jesus says the last shall be first (Matthew 19:30).

COMPETITION IN DIFFERENT WAYS

Children's Games ■ Involve everyone in games which they played when they were much younger. Offer good prizes for the winners to motivate everyone. Possible games could include Ring around the Rosey, Red Rover, Blind Man's Bluff, Pin the Tail on the Donkey, and Musical Chairs.

Losers Are Winners ■ Design contests which emphasize as positive those qualities which are usually thought of as negative. For example, the slowest in a race or the person with the least number of points could win.

No Control ■ Design contests where winners and losers really have no way to control the results. For example, they could be judged on physical characteristics (the tallest, oldest, blondest, one with brownest eyes, etc.).

Discussion Questions
- **How did you feel about the games tonight?**
- **Why were they different that the ones we usually play?** (They stressed qualities over which we have no control or which are usually seen as weaknesses or as immature.)
- **Do our usual games discriminate against anyone?** (Those who don't have natural physical abilities, etc.)
- **How does competition motivate you?**
- **How do you feel when you lose?**
- **Which people are labeled losers in our society?** (Poor people, old people, the disabled.)
- **Jesus said, "I tell you the truth, whatever you did for one of the least of these brothers of mine, you did for me"** (Matthew 25:31-46). **What does He mean, and how does His statement relate to our discussion?**

Wrap-up
1. Our society puts on a pedestal those who have natural physical endowments: beauty, strength, speed, and others. Those who are plain-looking or poor or who have the "wrong" race or social background are seen as losers.
2. The Bible warns us about how we treat the outcasts of the world. James 2:1-13 points out that we are guilty of sin in this area, even in church, when we defer to the person with money and fine clothes.
3. As we saw in Matthew, Jesus speaks very directly and emphatically about our treatment of the hungry, poor, and imprisoned. If our Christianity means anything at all, it must motivate us to reach out in love to others, despite the personal cost in dollars, time, and reputation.
4. Many Americans today will be like the rich man in Luke 16:19-31. Because he spent all his time accumulating treasure on earth, he lost heaven. Lazarus, the poor beggar, "won" in the end.

GAME OF GAMES

Explain that the object of the game is to win the most games. Divide into teams of two (ideally, boy-girl combinations). Then explain that throughout the house or church there are games in which they will compete. These games have been numbered. Each team will be given a piece of paper listing the order in which they will play the games. If you have 5 games (numbered 1 through 5), the teams would play each one at least once and, ideally, against different teams each time. The games could include Ping-Pong, pool, darts, penny-pitching, ring toss, bean bag tic-tac-toe, and shuffleboard (whatever the home or church has available). If only a few of these are available, design some of your own, using your imagination and inexpensive props. Each game should last about 5 minutes. Each time you blow the whistle, the teams move to their next locations and begin immediately. Whoever has the most points when the whistle blows wins the game they were playing. The final winning team should be determined by the number of winning points (6 points for a win, 4 points for a tie, 2 points for a loss). Be sure to offer very good prizes for the winning couple.

Discussion Questions
- **How did you feel about the games?**
- **What motivated you to compete?**
- **When and why were you tempted to cheat?**
- **How did you feel about the people against whom you were competing?**
- **In each game did you feel better about doing well or about doing better than the opposition? Why?**
- **When do you feel that life is a game like we played tonight?**

Wrap-up
1. To win tonight, you did not have to do well—only better than the opposition. Competition, therefore, does not always motivate a person to do his or her best. It may simply inspire cheating or doing just enough to win.
2. Competition can give a person a false sense of his or her worth. These were silly games; and yet each time you won, you felt like you had really accomplished something. Often we spend our lives winning trivial contests and ignoring major considerations. (See Matthew 23:23-24.)
3. God does not judge us on the basis of our performance. The good news of the Gospel is that no one can earn God's favor (Romans 3:10-23 and Ephesians 2:8-9). He accepts us as we are and offers salvation, free.

12

MUSIC

CROWD-BREAKERS

Air Band ■ Have a group of students lip sync and pantomine the movements to a rock song. This will take practice but can be very entertaining, especially if it's done well and doesn't drag on and on.

Fashionable ■ Bring a few bags full of clothes, make-up, and wigs. Group students in teams of four to six, and have them choose a person whom they will dress like a popular rock star. Have the stars parade one at a time in front of the crowd while the audience tries to guess their identity.

Finish This Sentence ■ These 10 great "doo-wop" phrases from rock music's early years are listed in *The Doo-Wop Sing-Along Songbook* (John Javna, St. Martin's Press). Print the first part of each phrase and see who can fill in the rest. Afterward, sing each of them for the group. Or you can use these as tongue-in-cheek examples of the meaningful words found in contemporary music. If the group protests that these songs are old and therefore are irrelevant examples, play a song from "In Visible Silence" by The Art of Noise or another example of computer-generated music.

1. Pa-pa-pa-pa-pa-pa-pa-oom-a-mow-mow, Papa-oom-mow-mow (from 'Papa-Oom-Mow-Mow" by the Rivingtons)
2. Bomp-ba-bomp-ba-ba-bomp, Ba-bom-ba-bom-bomp, Ba-ba-bomp-ba-ba-bomp, A-dang-a-dang-dang, A-ding-a-dong-ding, Bluuuue moooon (from 'Blue Moon" by the Marcels)
3. Oop-shoop, Shang-a-lack-a-cheek-a-bock (from "Remember Then" by the Earls)
4. Wop-wop, Doodly-wop. Wop-wop. Wop-wop, Doodly-wop. Wop-wop (from "At My Front Door" by the El Dorados)

108

5. Hoodly-papa-kow, Papa-kow, Papa-kow, Hoodly-papa-kow, Papa-kow, Papa-kow (from "I Promise to Remember" by Frankie Lymon & the Teenagers)
6. Rama-lama-lama-lama-lama-ding-dong, Rama-lama-lama-lama-lama-lama-ding (from "Rama Lama Ding Dong" by the Edsels)
7. Rang-tang-ding-dong, Rankety-sank (from "Rang Tang Ding Dong [I Am the Japanese Sandman]" by the Cellos)
8. Yip, Yip, Yip, Yip, Boom, Sha-na-na-na, Sha-na-na-na-na (from "Get a Job" by the Silhouettes)
9. Sho-dot'n shoby-doh, Sho-dot'n shoby-doh (from "In the Still of the Night" by the Five Satins)
10. Sho-be-doo-wop-wah-da (last line in "What's Your Name" by Don and Juan)

Here's the Pitch ■ Using a pitch pipe, give each section of the room a pitch to hum so that when humming together they make a chord. Explain that you are the "hum director" and that everyone should follow your direction. Review the choral directions for getting louder or softer, for raising or lowering the pitch one note, and for cutting them off. Make sure they are warmed up and that each group has the pitch, and then begin the "concert." Start slowly, with one group humming at a time, then softly form the chord. As you continue to direct, be creative, quieting one section while increasing the volume of another. Finish by raising the whole group a couple of pitches and with a loud crescendo, then cut them off with a grand flourish. This may also be effective with selected individuals seated in front of the group and singing "la."

I'll Make You a Star ■ Distribute old magazines, scissors, and tape and give everyone five minutes to create a "rock star" by tearing out body parts, clothes, musical instruments, etc., from the magazines and taping them together. They should also give their "stars" names. If there's time, have them make a rock group. Have the "stars" displayed and explained.

In Other Words ■ With the rise of Christian music, various attempts have been made to put Christian words to secular songs. An example of this is "Amazing Grace" sung to "The House of the Rising Sun" or to "The Happy Wanderer." Compose some of your own—they can be sublime or ridiculous. Use hymnals to find the words. For example, you could sing "Just As I Am" to "The Happy Wanderer" or you could put new words to the theme from "Moonlighting," etc. Another option would be to do this in groups and then have the groups perform for everyone.

Music Work ■ Many of the popular songs over the years have featured working or jobs as their theme. Hand out this quiz and let your kids match song title with artist. The correct answers are in parentheses.

MUSIC WORK

Song	Artist
_____ "Too Much Monkey Business" (k)	a. Sam Cooke
_____ "Get a Job" (d)	b. Jimmy Reed
_____ "Working In the Coal Mine" (h)	c. Donna Summer
_____ "Workin' for the Man" (j)	d. Silhouettes
_____ "Big Boss Man" (b)	e. Johnny Paycheck
_____ "Take This Job and Shove It" (e)	f. Wilson Pickett

____ "Boss Guitar" (i)	g. Dolly Parton
____ "She Works Hard For the Money" (c)	h. Lee Dorsey
____ "9 to 5" (g)	i. Duane Eddy
____ "Chain Gang" (a)	j. Roy Orbison
____ "Funk Factory (f)	k. Chuck Berry

You could create a similar quiz for other subjects such as love, weather, geography, girls' names, etc.

Name That Tune ■ Before the meeting, record a few bars of a variety of songs including rock, country, easy listening, oldies, show tunes, hymns, and contemporary Christian.

Divide into teams. For every song, each team should send up a contestant to be seated in front. Explain that you will play a song and the contestants should try to guess what it is. Whoever thinks he or she knows the answer should stand; the first person to stand gets the chance to "name that tune." Award 1000 points for every correct answer and -500 points for every incorrect one. As a variation, you can do this as individuals or couples and award good prizes to the winner(s); you could play "name the artist" instead.

Oldies But Goodies ■ Before the meeting, ask kids to bring old, throw-away records that they wouldn't mind destroying. Collect these records as the kids enter the room.

Divide into teams and give each team a stack of records and the assignment of creating a game for the whole group using these old, disposable records. After a few minutes, have each team explain their game to the whole group, and play it. If they draw a blank, here are a few suggestions:
1. "Thread the Records"—the first team to thread 10 records on a cord wins.
2. "Roll the Rock"—mark a goal and see who can roll a record the closest to it.
3. "The Record-Breaking Feet"—have a race between team representatives to see who can break a record the quickest using only his or her feet.
4. "Puzzled"—see who can piece together broken records the fastest.
5. "A Record Toss"—see who can throw the records like frisbees closest to a goal or in a garbage can some distance away.

Rhythm Band ■ Pass out a variety of strange and unusual instruments, noise-makers, and percussion possibilities. Choose a song, work out the parts, and perform it together. Possible instruments could include a kazoo, pitch pipe, bell, child's xylophone or piano, wooden blocks, pan lids, sandpaper, and others. Supplement these with mouth sounds.

Singing Challenge ■ Divide into teams. Using a "Top 40" list and other sources of songs (hymnal, *Campus Life* magazine, children's songbook, etc.), have a contest. For every round, each team should send one contestant to you. You will show them a song title and send them back to their teams. They are to sing the song without using the words in the title until their team guesses the correct title. The first team to correctly identify the song title wins that round. Remember, songs must be sung.

Tune That Name ■ Divide into teams, assign each team a fictitious song title, and give them a few minutes to write a song for it. Then have each group perform its song for the whole group. Here are some possible song titles.

- "Gimmie, Gimmie, Jimmy"
- "You are the Most . . ."
- "Down in the Dumps over You"
- "I Ache, I Pine, I Really Whine"
- "The Late Great Family Blues"
- "Love in the Ruins"
- "Shake and Break"
- "Over and Over and Over and Over and Over"
- "Etcetera"
- "Umph, Yeah, Wow, Oooh, Hmmm!"

Video Craze ■ Before the meeting, make a music video starring at least 10 or 12 kids. During the meeting, announce that you have taped a top video off MTV which you will be showing and which they should discuss as a group. Tell them to watch and listen carefully for the subtle nuances and blatant messages (especially listening for "backward masking"). Then run the tape. Another possibility would be to make a video in the meeting. Let group members know ahead of time and tell them what to bring for clothing, props, etc. Be sure to have your music and "concept" well thought through and prepared so that you don't waste time.

You'll Change Your Tune ■ This will involve a guest artist, someone who is proficient on the piano or guitar. Have him or her prepare a popular song or another familiar one to be performed in a variety of styles. The styles could include classic, opera, jazz, country, disco, punk, rock 'n' roll, blues, gospel, etc. The music group "Glad" does this in "Variations on a Hymn" (on the album "No Less Than All" from Milk and Honey Records).

DISCUSSION STARTERS

Archeology ■ Call your meeting "Raiders of the Lost D.J.," "E.T.'s Report," "Max Headroom Review," or another similar name. To set up your discussion, explain that archeologists in the future have found a tape which has 10 to 15 minutes of typical radio programming.The students should put themselves into the role of those future archeologists and try to discover as much as they can about the culture, beliefs, values, and habits of the earth people of the late twentieth century. Play the music (you can make the tape or just turn on the radio to the station to which everyone listens) and discuss what they hear.

Background ■ Purchase a "sampler record" from a Christian recording company and play it for your group as part of the meeting or as background music during refreshments. This will give a good introduction to Christian music. Also, show them the record reviews in *Campus Life* magazine.

Another option is to go to a Christian concert as a group and to discuss the experience afterward or at your next meeting. You could ask about the differences between this concert and a secular one, the "ministry" of the artist(s), the appropriateness of the price of admission, etc.

Christian Music ■ Play a couple of secular rock songs and a couple of Christian rock songs. Then ask:
- **Which songs were "Christian rock"? How could you tell?**
- **What makes songs "Christian" or "non-Christian"?**

■ **How do the following elements affect the "Christian-ness" of a song: beat, words, volume, motive for writing and/or performance, lifestyle of the performer, effects on the hearers, use of the money made?**

Compose Yourself ■ Pass out paper and pencils and tell everyone that they are going to write their own songs. They should begin by writing song lyrics. After a few minutes, have them read their lyrics aloud. Discuss the words and the type of music that would fit, then try to come up with a tune. It would help to have a couple of guitarists available. The songs don't have to be great compositions—the fun and meaning will come from the composition process and the discussion of which music will best fit the feel of the words.

Cover-up ■ Before the meeting, collect a number of album covers from a variety of popular rock groups. During the meeting, bring them out one at a time and analyze them together—both the pictures and the words printed on them. Ask how the covers match up to Christian values and biblical principles.

■ **Do they reflect the "works of the flesh" or the "fruit of the Spirit"?**
■ **Do they focus on what is good and pure?**
■ **Would listening to or singing this be glorifying to God?**
■ **Would these performers and their songs help their thought-life to be pleasing to God or to hinder it?**

Emphasize that you are not on a crusade to have them burn all their records or to have them listen only to "Christian" music. You are, however, telling them that they have the responsibility to be discerning with what they watch, hear, and buy. Reiterate the biblical principles implied by the questions above and encourage the kids to go home and analyze their records in light of them. Challenge them to pray for the courage to do what they know is right.

Hot and Heavy ■ Get the latest copy of *Billboard* magazine, in which the top-selling records in a variety of categories (including rock, gospel, soul, easy listening, country, and contemporary Christian) are listed.

Then design a matching quiz with the song titles on one side of the paper and the artists on the other. Mix in a few phony titles and artists to make the quiz more interesting and difficult (e.g., "You're My Hairy Carrie Bearie" by T.T. and the Tramps, "I've Been So Lonely in the Saddle Since My Horse Died" by Jimmy Bob Surefoot, "Slow Soul Sister" by Heavy Dude, "Momma Don't Teach!" by Moronna, and "The Lord's Drivin' and I'm Buckled Up" by Miss Dolly Would).

After you give the correct answers and declare the winner, involve the group members in a discussion of what it takes to sell a song, what music their friends like, how their tastes differ or are similar to what is popular, and the role music plays in their lives.

Media ■ Prepare a tape of song clips which reflect a variety of moods and values. Use a number of types of music including country, pop, easy listening, rock, heavy metal, and contemporary Christian. Prepare a slide show to coincide with the words or moods of the music.

Afterward, discuss what the kids felt and saw, what the songs tell us about ourselves and our society, and their other messages.

Questionnaire ■ Print this questionnaire (leaving plenty of space for answers) and distribute it in the meeting. After everyone fills it out, compile the answers and discuss the results.

Q & A

1. What word(s) most closely describes your taste in music? (Circle all that apply.)

tasteless	heavy metal	disco	hard rock
soft rock	big band	punk	easy listening
new wave	classical	muzak	hard-of-hearing
bubble gum	dentist office	jazz	oldies-but-goodies
Christian	computer	comedy	country/western

2. What three bands or musicians would you most pay to go hear?

3. What bands do you think should be paid to keep quiet?

4. If someone stole your entire record collection and the insurance company would give you the money for a whole new collection, what five albums would be at the top of your list to buy?

   Why?

5. What band or musician have you listened to and liked the longest?

6. What song title best describes your life?

7. What song best describes your school?

Resources ■ You may want to consider having an in-depth seminar on music or at least making available additional materials. Here are some resources.
■ Menconi Ministries (P.O. Box 306, Cardiff, CA 92007-0831; 619-436-8676). They have a regular newsletter and extensive material on popular music.
■ Dan and Steve Peters (Box 9222, North Saint Paul, MN 55109; 612-770-8114). They hold hard-hitting seminars on rock music, have written *Why Knock Rock*, *AC/DC—Wanted for Murder,* and other books, and have a video.
■ Bobby Dee, director of "Teen Vision" (Box 4505, Pittsburgh, PA 15205; 412-921-2400), puts out a very helpful newsletter by the same name. He also holds seminars on rock music.
■ Parents' Music Resource Center (1500 Arlington Blvd., Suite 300, Arlington, VA 22209). The center was begun by a group of congressional wives and has many helpful materials including a video, *Rising to the Challenge,* and a booklet, *Let's Talk Rock, a Primer for Parents.*
■ The film *Echoes* by Word, Inc.
■ The music section of *Campus Life* magazine gives helpful record reviews.

Top 40 ■ Pick up a number of "Top 40" lists from a local record store. Distribute them and analyze the songs together. Here are some possible characteristics to discuss.
■ Subjects (love, sex, school, society, religion . . .)
■ Style (rock, disco, ballad, folk, country, punk . . .)

- Singers (solo, group, instrumental, clean-cut, punk, rock-junkie, jock, men and women . . .)
- Subtleties (love is everything; do your own thing; sex is OK; love hurts; other hidden messages)
  Ask:
1. **What are the tendencies?**
2. **Based on this information, how would you write a surefire hit song?**
3. **Look at the list again. What are your favorite songs in the Top 40? Why do you like them?**
4. **What are your favorites which aren't listed?**
5. **How do our musical tastes reflect what's important to us?**

DISCUSSIONS

Stars and Real People ■ Read a portion of a recent interview with a Christian artist. These are available in *Contempory Christian* magazine or *Campus Life* magazine. Then ask:
1. **What do you think this person is really like?**
2. **Why do you think we put performers on "pedestals" and expect them to be "bigger than life?"** (Possible answers: their ad images; we need people to look up to.)
3. **How could putting people on pedestals hurt us?** (Possible answers: we follow their lead; when they fall, we're crushed; we should keep our eyes on Christ.)
4. **Does it help to know that Christian artists and stars are normal people?**
5. **Apply these questions to secular artists (e.g., Van Halen, Dolly Parton, Ozzie Osbourne, Tina Turner, Bon Jovi, etc.).**
6. **As a Christian, how do you feel about the "real people" listed in question number 5?**

Survey ■ Before the meeting, write out the following questions on separate pieces of paper. Give each person a slip of paper with a question on it. Then have them divide into twos and have each person ask his or her partner the question on the paper. (They should write down the answers.) After a few minutes, bring everyone back together and find out how the questions were answered. As the answers are reported, see if anyone has anything else to add, if they agree or disagree, how they feel about the question, etc. Here are the questions:
1. Who is you favorite recording individual or group? Why?
2. How many records or tapes do you own? How do you choose which ones to buy?
3. What is your favorite popular (top 40) song? What do the words mean?
4. What is the raunchiest song that you know that is now or was just recently very popular? What do the words mean?
5. What do you think of rating albums like they do with movies?
6. How do you think music affects your values, lifestyle, thought-life, and ideas?

The Music in Me ■ Ask:
- **What do you think about the words of the popular music these days? Do you listen to the words? Can you sing along with most songs?**
- **How do you think these words affect you? Do they turn you on? Change your ideas? Raise or lower your moral standards?**

114

■ What would other people think of you from your tastes in music? From your values, thought-life, personality, habits?

BIBLE STUDIES

Garbage In ■ Have everyone turn to Philippians 4:8. Read the verse aloud. Read aloud the first half of Proverbs 23:7 from the *New American Standard Bible.* Ask:
1. How do these verses relate to music—what we listen to, the words, etc?
2. In computer terms, GIGO, or "Garbage In, Garbage Out," means that what is fed into the computer is directly related to what comes out. How do you think this relates to the verses we just read?
3. What can we do to develop Christian listening habits?

Verses Versus ■ Distribute worksheets with the following Scripture references printed on them (print out the entire passage from a recent version like *The Living Bible).* After each one, have the students write how this passage should affect their music listening and buying habits.
1. Galatians 5:16-24
2. Philippians 4:8
3. 1 Corinthians 10:31
4. Psalm 19:14
   After everyone has finished, briefly discuss their answers, emphasizing the responsibility of Christians to be discerning in their listening habits.

13

EASTER

CROWD-BREAKERS

Bunny Hunt ■ Take one volunteer staff member dressed in a rented bunny suit (not Playboy style) with a large bag of miniature Easter eggs (wrapped). Add as many kids as possible—perhaps from other youth groups too. Mix them in a shopping mall or an enclosed public area. Divide the kids into teams of 10, and give the bunny a two-minute head start. Then send the teams in search of the bunny. Their objective is to pick up the trail of eggs and to track down the bunny within 20 minutes. The winners are either the bunny-nappers or the team collecting the most eggs.

Warning: Don't attempt this in a crowded mall or in wet weather (soggy bunnies don't hop too well).

For added fun, have an extra bunny appear at the opposite end of the mall to divert attention and to add confusion.

Be sure to have the bunny run along a prearranged path and to notify storekeepers and security guards.

Have the finale at a quiet section of the mall, an empty store, or a public podium for an Easter program.

Easter Parade ■ This is a team event. Give each team a bag of materials from which to fashion a very creative Easter bonnet. Include an old cap or hat, feathers, cloth, safety pins, paper and crayons, thread, cotton balls, yarn, old jewelry, etc.

Allow about 10 minutes for designing and creating the bonnets; then hold a fashion show for which each team chooses a model to wear the bonnet and an announcer who describes the creation while it is paraded around the room. Designate a runway area like in a beauty pageant, if you like.

Award a prize to the team with the most original bonnet and use them all in another activity (e.g., **Musical Bonnets**).

Egg Hunt ■ Have an old-fashioned Easter egg hunt. Collect or purchase quite a few plastic eggs (or use "L'eggs" stocking containers). Place slips of paper in them with various prizes or points. Hide them in a park or a large backyard the night before your meeting. Tell everyone to bring his or her own creative basket. At your signal, everyone should run to find as many eggs as possible. Award prizes for the most eggs, the most points, and the best basket.

Eggles ■ Use real eggs (hard-boiled) or pieces of cardboard cut into egg shapes. Also have available appropriate coloring and design items and utensils. Give everyone an egg and have them create "eggles." These are puns using eggs. Here are some examples: bald eggle, bold eggle, byc-eggle, med-eggle, mus-eggle, madri-eggle, mag-eggle.

Egg Roll ■ Choose as many teams as you wish for this relay, but be sure to arrange the team areas on all sides of the room. This will make the race much more interesting.

Give each team one large, plastic egg, taped so that the halves won't separate. At your signal, the first members from each team should roll their eggs on the floor with their noses, across the room and back. The next team members then repeat the process. To speed up the game, use only a few kids from each team or give them a shorter distance to roll. The first team finished wins.

Eggs-am ■ Explain that eggs are an integral part of any Easter celebration; therefore, you want to see how much they really know about eggs. Distribute the following quiz. (The answers are in parentheses.)

EGGS-AM FOR EGGHEADS

Write the "egg-word" to the right of the definition.

 1. check closely—   (eggs-amine)
 2. leave—   (eggs-it)
 3. precisely—   (eggs-actly)
 4. beautiful—   (eggs-quisite)
 5. of highest quality—   (eggs-cellent)
 6. a model—   (eggs-ample)
 7. to do very well—   (eggs-cel)
 8. to encourage—   (eggs-hort)
 9. someone who gets rid of demons—   (eggs-orcist)
10. to use up—   (eggs-pend)
11. to work hard—   (eggs-ert)
12. costly—   (eggs-pensive)
13. the end—   (eggs-tremity)
14. to work out—   (eggs-ercise)
15. to make larger than it is—   (eggs-aggerate)
16. add one of your own

After a few minutes, give the correct answers and see what new words they created.

Garden ■ Choose competitors to come to the front. Explain that one of the sure signs of spring is gardening and flowers. To have a good garden, however, you need a number of things. Their job is to find as many of these garden "things" as possible in three minutes. The "things" are listed for them. They should use their imaginations to find these items, and they must find everything in the room. They can use people, clothes, contents of purses and wallets, etc. Then give each of them a copy of the list (printed below) and tell them to begin. Afterward, have them display their gardening things and explain how they fit the categories on the list. Give a chocolate bunny to each of them and a prize to the winner.

GARDEN THINGS
1. roots
2. light
3. beauty
4. green
5. tool
6. growth
7. new leaf
8. soil
9. food
10. moisture

Hopping Contest ■ Choose competitors for an special Easter contest. After they come forward, bring out sets of "bunny ears." These should be made of cardboard with a string or rubber band so they can be placed on top of the head and the string tied under the chin. Introduce your bunnies to the crowd and explain that they are going to have a contest to see which bunny can hop the farthest. Mark out a starting line and explain that they each get three consecutive hops, starting behind the line, from a full stop. If they fall during the hops, where they hit will be the point from which the distance is measured. The winner will be the bunny who hops the farthest with his or her three consecutive hops. (This is like a combination of the standing long jump and hop, skip, and jump.) Have the bunnies compete one at a time. Then give a chocolate bunny to each competitor and a prize to the winner.

Magic Egg ■ Recruit a number of competitors to see who can get a hard-boiled egg into a milk bottle. Here's how it's done: boil an egg; peel the egg; place the egg over the mouth of a milk bottle (it will not go in); remove the egg; light a paper taper and place it in the bottle. When it is extinguished, place the egg on the bottle and watch it get sucked into the bottle (the vacuum pulls it in).

Musical Bonnets ■ Bring all sorts of hats so that you have enough for everyone. Form the group in a large circle with everyone wearing a hat except for one person. Play a song like "Here Comes Peter Cottontail" or another similar rendition. As the music is played, the hats must move from head to head. (Each person uses the right hand to remove the hat and place it on the head of the person to the right.) To complicate matters, you can call **Switch!** and have the hats move to the left with the left hands. When the music stops, whoever is hatless is eliminated. Then remove another bonnet and continue. The winner is the last person left with a bonnet on his or her head.

New Wave ■ Using the whole group (make sure that everyone is seated), hold your own indoor version of the famous "wave cheer." (The wave cheer is a chain-reaction event. The first person stands and cheers. He or she just rises slowly and then sits back down slowly. Right after he or she begins, the next person begins, and so on. The crowd undulates, like a wave, as the movement and sound travel across or around the room.) Begin at one side of the room and have kids stand, raise their hands high over their heads, and blow noisemakers. Go from one side of the room to the other and back (direct them if it will help). Then, try it in a circle with everyone seated around you.

Party Hardy ■ Have an Easter "party." Beforehand, decorate the room with streamers, balloons, etc., to give it a party atmosphere. Provide paper party hats and noisemakers to blow into. (Try to have four different kinds of noisemakers—horns, whistles, "dragon's tongues," kazoos, etc.) As kids enter the room, give each one a hat and a noisemaker. After most of the crowd has arrived, explain that for the next half hour whenever any latecomer enters the room you will say, **HEY!** and they should stand and shout, **SURPRISE!** and blow their noisemakers. (See **Surprises** for the tie-in.) They should do this no matter what activity they are doing. Then tell them to get with all the others with their particular noisemaker and sit on the floor.

Explain that you are forming a special Easter band, and they have the instruments. Each group is a section of the band. Then, with you as the director, lead them in an instrumental rendition of "Here Comes Peter Cottontail." Be sure to point to specific groups for a few measures or to individuals for solos, and direct them, with great flourish of course, to play louder or softer. Do another song as a whole band, or give each section a few minutes to decide on a song what they will play for everyone else. Then have the sections play one at a time.

Surprises ■ Between games, have "surprises" for everyone. These will have to be lined up in advance. They tie into the idea that Easter caught the disciples by surprise and today the resurrection still catches people by surprise.
■ Surprise #1—Have someone turn off the lights and yell loudly, **Help, help! I'm drowning!** After a few seconds, he or she should turn on the lights. Proceed with the meeting as though nothing unusual has happened.
■ Surprise #2—Get everyone quiet and begin to give announcements or to explain the next activity. Have two kids (one on each side and behind the crowd) pull "party poppers" simultaneously. Proceed as though nothing has happened and go on with the next game.
■ Surprise #3—Have a boy burst into the room, through the crowd, and to the front yelling, **Woman the lifeboats! Woman the lifeboats! Woman the lifeboats!** Stop him and say, **Wait a minute—it's not "woman the lifeboats," it's "man the lifeboats."** He then should respond, **You fill 'em your way, and I'll fill 'em mine!**

The Egg Bowl ■ Use teams or team representatives and have a contest like the "College Bowl" or "Prep Bowl" quiz games on television. When anyone knows the answer to a question, he or she should stand. The first person standing will have the first opportunity to answer the question. Each correct answer receives 1000 points and each incorrect answer receives -2000 points. After an incorrect answer, one other person will have the opportunity to give the correct one. Appoint a judge to keep track of the points and begin. Here are the questions—the answers are in parentheses.
1. Where did Peter Cottontail hop? (down the bunny trail)
2. For "Daylight Savings Time," which way do we set our clocks? (ahead, one hour)
3. Who is the male MC for the Easter Seals telethon? (Pat Boone)

4. In the song, where did they wear their "Easter bonnets"? ("in the Easter parade")
5. In Tiny Tim's famous song, what did he tiptoe through? (the tulips)
6. In what ocean is Easter Island? (South Pacific)
7. What is the "vernal equinox"? (the first day of spring, when day and night are of equal length)
8. Why did the chicken sit in the middle of the road? (She wanted to "lay it on the line.")
9. Name 3 early spring flowers. (daffodils, tulips, crocuses, etc.)
10. What charity has Easter Seals? (the American Lung Association)
11. What did Peter Cottontail get caught eating in Mr. McGregor's garden? (cabbage)
12. What's at the bottom of almost every Easter basket? (grass)
13. What returns to Capistrano in the spring? (swallows)
14. What comes in like a lion and goes out like a lamb? (March)
15. What are the Easter colors? (pink, purple, and white)
16. Name three famous bunnies. (Bugs Bunny, Crusader Rabbit, Peter Cottontail, Easter Bunny, Brer Rabbit, Trix bunny, Flopsy, Mopsy, Rabbit Stew, etc.)
17. What professional baseball team has spring training in Vero Beach, Florida? (the Los Angeles Dodgers)
18. How many days does April have? (30)
19. When should people plant tulip bulbs if they want them to come up in the spring? (late fall)
20. Where was the "final four" held in 1988? (Kansas City)

DISCUSSION STARTERS

Action ■ Give everyone the assignment of asking four or five Christian adults what they would think if someone discovered the bones of Jesus. What difference would it make to their faith? Discuss the answers at the next meeting.

Easter Cards ■ Explain that Easter is the greatest Christian holiday because the Resurrection is the final, indisputable proof that Jesus is who He said He was and that His death on the cross really was for our sins. Ask them to think for a moment of a non-Christian friend to whom they could send special Easter greetings—just to be nice or perhaps even to help share the Gospel with this person. Then bring out card-making materials, including construction paper, white paper, felt-tipped pens of various colors, magazines from which they can tear pictures, cotton balls, scissors, tape, glue, etc. Allow about 10 minutes for everyone to make their cards, and then have them displayed for the rest of the group. Encourage them to deliver them personally or to mail them to their special friends.

Eyewitnesses ■ Before the meeting, line up people to play the characters below. The actors should learn the lines well enough to deliver them dramatically. During the meeting, explain that despite all the bunnies and eggs, Easter really should center on Christ. There were men and women who witnessed Jesus' arrest and crucifixion, and these eyewitnesses are here to tell the story. (Note: Before each eyewitness speaks, read the appropriate passage from the Bible. Then the actor should deliver the lines as printed below.)
1. Soldier (Matthew 27:27-30, 35-37, 54)
   I watched Him die. Actually, all three of them . . . but Him I'll remember. He

120

screamed out something about God . . . I got closer. Then He whispered something about forgiveness . . . that we didn't know what we were doing. And then He died—just like that—early. Oh, He was dead all right. We made sure of that. But I'll never forget His face or what He said. I've seen plenty of executions, but none like that . . . or Him.

2. Disciple (Matthew 26:31, 33-35, 43-46, 49-50, 56b)
   I followed him for three years. We walked, ate, and talked together. He was quite a man . . . He changed my life. But I'll never forget that night. Yes, I was there in the garden. I had said that I would die for Him, but when all those guards came, I ran away to save my life just like the rest. Then I followed at a distance and watched the phony trial and the way they mocked Him. They gave Him the death penalty and pounded nails through His hands and feet and shoved that monstrous cross in the ground. I loved that man. But when He died, I left . . . in despair. He was dead, and all that I had hoped for died with Him.

3. Guard (Matthew 27:62-66)
   I was there too—at the trial before the chief priests and the others. I hated Him—all that talk about forgiving sins, destroying the temple . . . and love. Who did he think He was—God? Anyway, I was there at the cross too, and I saw Him die—and I knew that finally we would be rid of this threat to our religion and way of life. Afterward, I was given a new assignment—to guard the tomb. I'm not sure why. Who would want to steal anything from that grave? He was poor, and all his followers had run away. I guess He had said something about coming back to life again, so the high priests wanted to stop any tricks or messing around. Well, they'll have to get through me and the others . . . and that stone!

4. Woman (Matthew 27:55-56)
   Please excuse my tears . . . but I was there . . . at the cross . . . and saw my Lord die. Like the others, I loved Him—He understood my struggles and feelings . . . and He gave me God's forgiveness for everything I had done. I guess it's all over now. I wonder what happened to Peter and Nathanael and James and the others.

   The crowds treated Him like a criminal—laughing, cursing, mocking Him. And where will He be buried? My Lord! What'll I do . . . what'll we do?"

After the eyewitnesses leave, walk to the front and say: **Yes, Jesus died—you've heard the eyewitness reports. He was crucified, dead, and buried in a borrowed tomb. And guards were posted and a huge stone rolled in front to keep him in that tomb. But let me read you the rest of the story.**

Then read Matthew 28:1-20 and make the following comments: **Jesus was dead, BUT HE AROSE! And the eyewitnesses to his death became eyewitnesses to His resurrection—the guards, the women, the disciples, and many others. This event, the Resurrection, changed lives . . . and history. Just consider the disciples. They were scattered, discouraged, and defeated. But suddenly they were bold, fearless, and confident. What changed them? They had seen Christ alive!**

Easter is more than bunnies, eggs, vacation, flowers, and spring—it is the celebration of our LIVING LORD! And here's what Christ's resurrection means to us. Because He rose from the dead and is alive . . .

1. **We know that He was and He is GOD—we have the proof.**
2. **We know that what He taught and promised is TRUE.**
3. **We know that He died for a reason—He died for our sins, in our place.**
4. **We know that He now lives to love us and to bring us to God.**

Conclude by challenging the students to worship Christ, the living Lord, and to give their lives to Him.

Grab Bag ■ Before the meeting, gather a number of small items and put them in a large garbage bag. Here are some possibilities: mirror, knife, stone, clock, picture frame, stuffed animal, handkerchief, stick, index card, soap, light bulb, hammer, paper clip, shirt, wallet, eraser, balloon, rubber band, carrot, newspaper, etc. Make sure that you have enough for every person; or, with a large crowd, use just those who didn't compete in the other games.

Explain that you want the participants to reach into the bag and pull something out. Then they should think of how that item symbolizes Easter for them. After everyone has drawn an item and had a few seconds to think, go around the room and have them explain their symbols quickly, one at a time. For example, someone could say: **The eraser reminds me of Easter because when Jesus died on the cross, He erased my sins.** Some of the answers may be light or humorous (e.g., the carrot could remind someone of a rabbit, etc.). That's all right. The purpose of this activity is to focus attention on Easter.

Jerusalem Star ■ As a group, work out a front page or two of a newspaper, *The Jerusalem Star,* as it would appear after the Resurrection. Assign articles, collect them, print the paper, and distribute it on Easter Sunday (with the pastor's permission, of course).

DISCUSSIONS

Meanings ■ Ask:
- **What is Easter really all about?**
- **Why is Christ's resurrection important?**
- **What difference should the Resurrection make in our lives today?**

Spring ■ Ask for a show of hands for those who really want springtime to come. Then ask:
- **What do you like about spring?** (warm weather, flowers, approaching end of school, special events, holidays, etc.)
- **What does spring mean?** (thawing, growing, planting, warming up, etc.)
- **What special traditions do you have for spring?** (Easter, ski trip, beach trip, prom, gardening, etc.)

Next, use the following words with personal applications. You may want to invite other suggestions as you go along.
- *Thaw*—means melting, unfreezing, etc. Besides ice and the ground, there are other things that need "thawing"—certain relationships, frozen attitudes, etc.
- *Plant*—Involves placing seeds or bulbs in the earth and watching them "come to life" as water and sun are added. There are many things which should be "planted" in our lives: love, faith, hope, concern, etc.
- *Grow*—maturing, getting bigger, developing. We should be growing in all sorts of ways: spiritually, socially, mentally, physically. It has been said that when you stop growing, you start dying.
- *Warm up*—Beyond just thawing, this means that the whole climate changes. Relationships, attitudes, life-goals, etc., all need to be "warmed up."

Next, hand out the following worksheets and ask the group to fill them out seriously and prayerfully.

I would like to "thaw" _____ .

I would like to "plant" _____ .

I would like to see "growth" in _____ .

I would like to "warm up" _____ .

Then have them pair up with anyone else in the room. Seat everyone and have them take a few minutes to share with each other what they wrote on their worksheets. Have them take two or three minutes to pray for each other.

Thoughts ■ Use the following as a wrap-up or a discussion guide.

■ The Resurrection is the most important event in history. If it is true, as Christians believe, then Jesus *is* God, His death *was* for our sins, and what we do with Him *has* eternal consequences. The Incarnation, grace, and eternal life are real.

■ If, however, Jesus did not rise from the dead, then Christians are the most foolish people in the world, and all the martyrs throughout history have died in vain.

■ But the Resurrection *did* occur. It was a historical, time-and-space event. It was not a "spiritual resurrection" or an "idea," but a real body, once dead, came back to life at a particular time. The historical evidence is there and cannot be denied. We have an empty tomb, and we worship a living Saviour.

BIBLE STUDIES

Predictions ■ Have everyone follow in their Bibles as you highlight the following situations where Jesus predicted His resurrection from the dead. You may want to discuss these as you move along. The idea is that the disciples were surprised by the Resurrection, *but they should not have been!* Jesus had told them a number of times that it would happen—for some reason, they didn't hear Him.

1. John 2:19-22—"Destroy this temple, and I will raise it again in three days." This is the statement which was used against Him at His trial.
2. Matthew 12:38-40 and 16:1-4—"For as Jonah was three days and three nights in the belly of a huge fish, so the Son of Man will be three days and three nights in the heart of the earth."
3. Matthew 16:21-23—"And on the third day be raised to life." Evidently the disciples heard only the part about His suffering and dying because Peter told Jesus that these things won't happen. Jesus rebuked Peter strongly.
4. Matthew 17:23—"And on the third day He will be raised to life." Again Jesus predicted His death and resurrection.

Today people are surprised by the Resurrection. They don't believe it really happened or that "rational" people can believe such a thing. What do you say to them? (Discuss briefly.)

Spring ■ Challenge your group to:

■ Spring up—"All of us must quickly carry out the tasks assigned us by the one who sent Me, for there is little time left before the night falls and all work comes to an end" (John 9:4, TLB). Don't lie around—get up and get busy—there's much to do!

- Spring forward—Paul says, "Forgetting the past and looking forward to what lies ahead, I strain to reach the end of the race and receive the prize for which God is calling us up to heaven because of what Christ Jesus did for us." (Philippians 3:13-14, TLB). Move ahead in your life and in your commitment to Christ. Don't be content with the status quo.
- Spring into action—Do you really believe in God? Then act like it. As James says, "Faith that does not result in good deeds is not real faith" (James 2:20, TLB). Look for ways to put your faith into action.

Witnesses ■ Hand out the following worksheet (leaving plenty of space for answers), and divide into four groups. Assign each group a section or two on which to work. After five minutes or so, bring them back together and have the groups report their findings. Everyone else can write down the answers in their empty sections.

EYEWITNESS NEWS

Passage	Witness(es)	Instructions (What did Jesus tell them to do?)
1. Matthew 28:1-20		
2. Mark 16:1-20		
3. Luke 24:1-53		
4. John 20:1-31		
5. John 21:1-25		
6. Acts 1:1-11		
7. 1 Corinthians 15:3-11		

Wrap-up ■ Read 1 Corinthians 15:12-28 and emphasize the importance of the Resurrection to our faith. Jesus rose *literally* (it actually happened in history) and *bodily* (it was a physical resurrection—not some sort of a "spiritual" happening).

Say something like: **The reality of the Resurrection turned the lives of the disciples upside down. From frightened and discouraged men and women, huddling in a room for comfort and safety, they were transformed into those who willingly gave up their lives for the Gospel—because they had seen the risen Christ, and they knew He was and is the Lord! Today, people are still surprised by the Resurrection, but we must tell them that it is true and that Christ lives. This Easter, let the reality of the Resurrection fill you with hope and with the determination to spread the news.**

MORE PROGRAMMING RESOURCES FROM SONPOWER

THE *ANY OLD TIME* SERIES

Any Old Time books give you ready-to-use, creative meeting plans that are strong on content and short on preparation time. Each volume includes 15 complete sessions, each with opening games and warm-up activities, practical and relevant Bible study, and a wrap-up section to help your teens remember and apply what they have learned. The sessions can be used independently—anytime and anywhere. Or they can be used in sequence to give your group weeks of challenging meetings.

Look for the *Any Old Time* series at your local Christian bookstore or order from SP Publications, 1825 College Ave., Wheaton, IL 60187.

ANY OLD TIME BOOK 1 *by David Veerman*
Youth programs from the leaders of Youth for Christ/USA on topics like drinking, dating, sex, witnessing, faith, peer pressure, and priorities.
6-2595

ANY OLD TIME BOOK 2 *by David Veerman*
More great meeting ideas from Youth for Christ leaders, on loneliness, self-acceptance, suicide, moral choices, prayer, parents, and more.
6-2596

ANY OLD TIME BOOK 3 *by Stan Campbell*
Sixteen sessions that can be used independently or as four separate four-part units on the themes of relationships, failure, "things you can't avoid," and modern-day myths.
6-2648

ANY OLD TIME BOOK 4 *by Stan Campbell*
Youth programs especially designed for holidays and special events: Christmas, Easter, New Year's, Halloween, Independence Day, Valentine's Day, church picnic, Thanksgiving Day, Labor Day, Mother's and Father's Day, graduation, and lock-ins.
6-2640

ANY OLD TIME BOOK 5 *by Paul Borthwick*
Four units of four sessions each that can be used independently or consecutively to involve young people in local and world outreach.
6-2187

ANY OLD TIME BOOK 6 *by David Veerman*
Creative meeting ideas organized around the themes of basic doctrines, Christian growth, Christian living, and relationships.
6-2510

ANY OLD TIME BOOK 7 *by David Veerman*
More meeting ideas from the leaders of Youth for Christ/USA, focusing on independent faith, the Resurrection and Second Coming, the goal of the Christian life, and more.
6-2560

ANY OLD TIME BOOK 8 *by Duffy Robbins*
Fifteen stand-alone meeting ideas that can also be used for three units on growth: as a person, as a disciple, and as a fellowship.
6-2514

ANY OLD TIME BOOK 9 *by Sandy Larsen*
Three units of five sessions each that can be used separately or in sequence to develop a servant's heart among students.
6-1360

ANY OLD TIME BOOK 10 *by David Veerman*
Fifteen more creative lesson ideas on conversion, effective prayer, consistent faith, and facing the future.
6-1454